PERSONALITY

LECTURES DELIVERED IN AMERICA

PERSONALITY

LECTURES DELIVERED
IN AMERICA

BY

SIR RABINDRANATH TAGORE

WITH ILLUSTRATIONS

GYAN

Published by

Gyan Publishing House
5, Ansari Road
Daryaganj, New Delhi-110002
Phone: 011-47034999, 9811692060
E-mail: books@gyanbooks.com

Distribution Network
gyanbooks.com
India, USA, Canada, UK, Australia

ISBN: 978-81-212-5689-6 (PB)
First Published, 1917

2nd Impression 2024

Printed at: Gyan Press, Delhi.

PERSONALITY LECTURES DELIVERED IN AMERICA
Author: RABINDRANATH TAGORE

PERSONALITY

AT SANTA BARBARA, CALIFORNIA

Frontispiece.

PERSONALITY

BY

SIR RABINDRANATH TAGORE

AUTHOR OF

"GITANJALI," "THE CRESCENT MOON," ETC.

New York

THE MACMILLAN COMPANY

1917

TO

C. F. ANDREWS

CONTENTS

LIST OF ILLUSTRATIONS

WHAT IS ART?

WHAT IS ART?

We are face to face with this great world and our relations to it are manifold. One of these is the necessity we have to live, to till the soil, to gather food, to clothe ourselves, to get materials from nature. And we are always making things that will satisfy our need, and we come in touch with Nature in our efforts to meet these needs. We are always in touch with this great world through hunger and thirst and all our physical needs.

Then we have our mind; and mind seeks its own food. Mind has its necessity also. It must find out reason in things. It is faced with a multiplicity of facts, and is bewildered when it cannot find one unifying principle which simplifies the heterogeneity of things. Man's constitution is such that he must not only find facts, but also some laws which will lighten the burden of mere number and quantity.

There is yet another man in me, not the physical, but the personal man; which has its likes and dislikes, and wants to find something to fulfil its needs of love. This personal man is found in the region where we are free from all necessity, — above the needs, both of body and mind, — above the expedient and useful. It is the highest in man, — this personal man. And it has personal relations of its own with the great world, and comes to it for something to satisfy personality.

The world of science is not a world of reality, it is an abstract world of force. We can use it by the help of our intellect but cannot realize it by the help of our personality. It is like a swarm of mechanics who, though producing things for ourselves as personal beings, are mere shadows to us.

But there is another world which is real to us. We see it, feel it; we deal with it with all our emotions. Its mystery is endless because we cannot analyze it or measure it. We can but say, "Here you are."

This is the world from which Science turns away, and in which Art takes its place. And if we can answer the question as to what art is, we shall know what this world is with which art has such intimate relationship

It is not an important question as it stands. For Art, like life itself, has grown by its own impulse, and man has taken his pleasure in it without definitely knowing what it is. And we could safely leave it there, in the subsoil of consciousness, where things that are of life are nourished in the dark.

But we live in an age when our world is turned inside out and where there is dragged to the surface whatever lies at the bottom. Our very process of living, which is an unconscious process, we must bring under the scrutiny of our knowledge, — even though to know is to kill our object of research and to make it a museum specimen.

Questions have been asked, "What is Art?" and answers have been given by various persons. These discussions are introducing elements of conscious purpose into the region where both our faculties of creation and enjoyment have been spontaneous and half-conscious. They are supplying us with very definite standards by which to guide our judgment of art productions. Therefore we have heard judges in the modern time giving verdict, according to some special legislature of their own make, for the dethronement of immortals whose supremacy has been unchallenged for centuries.

This meteorological disturbance in the atmosphere of art criticism, whose origin is in the West, has crossed over to our own shores in Bengal, bringing mist and clouds in its wake, where there was a clear sky. We have begun to ask ourselves whether creations of art should not be judged either according to their fitness to be universally understood, or their philosophical interpretation of life, or their usefulness for solving the problems of the day, or their giving expression to something which is peculiar to the genius of the people to which the artist belongs. Therefore when men are seriously engaged in fixing the standard of value in art by something which is not inherent in it, — or in other words when the excellence of the river is going to be judged by the point of view of a canal, we cannot leave the question to its fate, but must take our part in the deliberations.

Should we begin with a definition? But definition of a thing which has a life growth is really limiting one's own vision in order to be able to see clearly. But clearness is not necessarily the only, or the most important, aspect of a truth. A bull's-eye lantern view is a clear view, but not a complete view. If we must know a wheel in motion, we should not mind if all its spokes cannot be counted. When not merely the accuracy of shape, but velocity of motion, is important, we have to be content with a somewhat imperfect definition of the wheel. Living things have far-reaching relationships with their surroundings, some of which are invisible and go deep down into the soil. In our zeal for definition we lop off branches and roots of a tree to turn it into a log, which is easier to roll about from classroom to classroom, and therefore suitable for a text-book. But because it allows a nakedly clear view of itself, it cannot be said that a log gives a truer view of a tree as a whole.

Therefore I shall not define Art, but question myself about the reason of its existence, and try to find out whether it owes its origin to some social purpose, or to the need of catering for our æsthetic enjoyment, or whether it has come out of some impulse of expression, which is the impulse of our being itself.

A fight has been going on for a long time round the saying, "Art for Art's sake," which seems to have fallen into disrepute among a section of Western critics. It is a sign of the recurrence of the ascetic ideal of the puritanic age, when enjoyment as an end in itself was held to be sinful. But all puritanism is a reaction. It does not represent truth in its normal aspect. When enjoyment loses its direct touch with life, growing fastidious and fantastic in its world of elaborate conventions, then comes the call for renunciation which rejects happiness itself as a snare. I am not going into the history of your modern art, which I am not at all competent to discuss; yet I can assert it, as a general truth, that when a man tries to thwart himself in his desire for delight, converting it merely into his desire to know, or to do good, then the cause must be that his power of feeling delight has lost its natural bloom and healthiness.

The rhetoricians in old India had no hesitation in saying, that enjoyment is the soul of literature, — the enjoyment which is disinterested. But the word "enjoyment" has to be used with caution. When analyzed, its spectrum shows an endless series of rays of different colours and intensity throughout its different worlds of stars. The art world contains elements which are distinctly its own and which emit lights that have their special range and property. It is our duty to distinguish them and come to their origin and growth.

The most important distinction between the animal and man is this, that the animal is very nearly bound within the limits of its necessities, the greater part of its activities being necessary for its self-preservation and preservation of race.

Like a retail shopkeeper, it has no large profit from its trade of life; the bulk of its earnings must be spent in paying back the interest to its bank. Most of its resources are employed in the mere endeavour to live. But man, in life's commerce, is a big merchant. He earns a great deal more than he is absolutely compelled to spend. Therefore there is a vast excess of wealth in man's life, which gives him the freedom to be useless and irresponsible to a great measure. There are large outlying tracts, surrounding his necessities, where he has objects that are ends in themselves.

The animals must have knowledge, so that their knowledge can be employed for useful purposes of their life. But there they stop. They must know their surroundings in order to be able to take their shelter and seek their food, some properties of things in order to build their dwellings, some signs of the different seasons to be able to get ready to adapt themselves to the changes. Man also must know because he must live. But man has a surplus where he can proudly assert that knowledge is for the sake of knowledge. There he has the pure enjoyment of his knowledge, because there knowledge is freedom. Upon this fund of surplus his science and philosophy thrive.

Then again, there is a certain amount of altruism in the animal. It is the altruism of parenthood, the altruism of the herd and the hive. This altruism is absolutely necessary for race preservation. But in man there is a great deal more than this. Though he also has to be good, because goodness is necessary for his race, yet he goes far beyond that. His goodness is not a small pittance, barely sufficient for a hand-to-mouth moral existence. He can amply afford to say that goodness is for the sake of goodness. And upon this wealth of goodness, — where honesty is not valued for being the best policy, but because it can afford to go against all policies, — man's ethics are founded.

The idea of "Art for Art's sake" also has its origin in this region of the superfluous. Let us, therefore, try to ascertain what activity it is, whose exuberance leads to the production of Art.

For man, as well as for animals, it is necessary to give expression to his feelings of pleasure and displeasure, fear, anger and love. In animals, these emotional expressions have gone little beyond their bounds of usefulness. But in man, though they still have roots in their original purposes, they have spread their branches far and wide in the infinite sky high above their soil. Man has a fund of emotional energy which is not all occupied in his self-preservation. This surplus seeks its outlet in the creation of Art, for man's civilization is built upon his surplus.

A warrior is not merely content with fighting, which is needful, but, by the aid of music and decorations, he must give expression to the heightened consciousness of the warrior in him, which is not only unnecessary, but in some cases suicidal. The man who has a strong religious feeling not only worships his deity with all care, but his religious personality craves, for its expression, the splendour of the temple, the rich ceremonials of worship.

When a feeling is aroused in our hearts which is far in excess of the amount that can be completely absorbed by the object which has produced it, it comes back to us and makes us conscious of ourselves by its return waves. When we are in poverty, all our attention is fixed outside us, — upon the objects which we must acquire for our need. But when our wealth greatly surpasses our needs, its light is reflected back upon us, and we have the exultation of feeling that we are rich persons. This is the reason why, of all creatures, only man knows himself, because his impulse of knowledge comes back to him in its excess. He feels more intensely his personality than other creatures, because his power of feeling is more than can be exhausted by his objects. This efflux of the consciousness of his personality requires an outpour of expression. Therefore, in Art, man reveals himself and not his objects. His objects have their place in books of information and science, where he has completely to conceal himself.

I know I shall not be allowed to pass unchallenged when I use the word "personality," which has such an amplitude of meaning. These loose words can be made to fit ideas which have not only different dimensions, but shapes also. They are like raincoats, hanging in the hall, which can be taken away by absent-minded individuals having no claim upon them.

Man, as a knower, is not fully himself,—his mere information does not reveal him. But, as a person, he is the organic man, who has the inherent power to select things from his surroundings for making them his own. He has his forces of attraction and repulsion by which he not merely piles up things outside him, but creates himself. The principal creative forces, which transmute things into our living structure, are emotional forces. A man, where he is religious, is a person, but not where he is mere theologian. His feeling for the divine is creative. But his mere knowledge of the divine cannot be formed into his own essence because of this lack of the emotional fire.

Let us here consider what are the contents of this personality and how it is related to the outer world. This world appears to us as an individual, and not merely as a bundle of invisible forces. For this, as everybody knows, it is greatly indebted to our senses and our mind. This apparent world is man's world. It has taken its special features of shapes, colours and movements from the peculiar range and qualities of our perception. It is what our sense limits have specially acquired and built for us and walled up. Not only the physical and chemical forces, but man's perceptual forces, are its potent factors, — because it is man's world, and not an abstract world of physics or metaphysics.

This world, which takes its form in the mould of man's perception, still remains only as the partial world of his senses and mind. It is like a guest and not like a kinsman. It becomes completely our own when it comes within the range of our emotions. With our love and hatred, pleasure and pain, fear and wonder, continually working upon it, this world is becoming a part of our personality. It grows with our growth, it changes with our changes. We are great or small, according to the magnitude and littleness of this assimilation, according to the quality of its sum total. If this world were taken away, our personality would lose all its content.

Our emotions are the gastric juices which transform this world of appearance into the more intimate world of sentiments. On the other hand, this outer world has its own juices, having their various qualities which excite our emotional activities. This is called in our Sanskrit rhetoric *rasa*, which signifies outer juices having their response in the inner juices of our emotions. And a poem, according to it, is a sentence or sentences containing juices, which stimulate the juices of emotion. It brings to us ideas, vitalized by feelings, ready to be made into the life-stuff of our nature.

Bare information of facts is not literature, because it gives us merely the facts which are independent of ourselves. Repetition of the fact that the sun is round, water is liquid, fire is hot, would be intolerable. But a description of the beauty of the sunrise has its eternal interest for us, — because there, it is not the fact of the sunrise, but ourselves, which is the object of perennial interest.

It is said in the Upanishat that "Wealth is dear to us, not because we desire the fact of the wealth itself, but because we desire ourselves." Its meaning is, that we feel ourselves in our wealth, — and therefore we love it. The things which arouse our emotions arouse our own self-feeling. It is like our touch upon the harp-string: if it is too feeble, then we are merely aware of the touch, but if it is strong, then our touch comes back to us in tunes and our consciousness is intensified.

There is the world of science, from which the elements of personality have been carefully removed. We must not touch it with our feelings.

But there is also the vast world, which is personal to us. We must not merely know it, and then put it aside, but we must feel it, — because, by feeling it, we feel ourselves.

But how can we express our personality, which we only know by feeling? A scientist can make known what he has learned by analysis and experiment. But what an artist has to say, he cannot express by merely informing and explaining. The plainest language is needed when I have to say what I know about a rose, but to say what I feel about a rose is different. There it has nothing to do with facts, or with laws, — it deals with taste, which can be realized only by tasting. Therefore the Sanskrit rhetoricians say, in poetry we have to use words which have got the proper taste, — which do not merely talk, but conjure up pictures and sing. For pictures and songs are not merely facts, — they are personal facts. They are not only themselves, but ourselves also. They defy analysis and they have immediate access to our hearts.

It has to be conceded, that man cannot help revealing his personality, also, in the world of use. But there self-expression is not his primary object. In everyday life, when mostly we are moved by our habits, we are economical in our expression; for then our soul-consciousness is at its low level, — it has just volume enough to glide on in accustomed grooves. But when our heart is fully awakened in love, or in other great emotions, our personality is in its flood-tide. Then it feels the longing to express itself for the very sake of expression. Then comes Art, and we forget the claims of necessity, the thrift of usefulness, — the spires of our temples try to kiss the stars and the notes of our music to fathom the depth of the ineffable

Man's energies, running on two parallel lines, — that of utility and of self-expression — tend to meet and mingle. By constant human associations sentiments gather around our things of use and invite the help of art to reveal themselves, — as we see the warrior's pride and love revealed in the ornamental sword blade, and the comradeship of festive gatherings in the wine goblet.

The lawyer's office, as a rule, is not a thing of beauty, and the reason is obvious. But in a city, where men are proud of their citizenship, public buildings must express this love for the city in their structures. When the British capital was removed from Calcutta to Delhi, there was discussion about the style of architecture which should be followed in the new buildings. Some advocated the Indian style of the Moghal period, — the style which was the joint production of the Moghal and the Indian genius. The fact that they lost sight of was that all true art has its origin in sentiment. Moghal Delhi and Moghal Agra show their human personality in their buildings. Moghal emperors were men, they were not mere administrators. They lived and died in India, they loved and fought. The memorials of their reigns do not persist in the ruins of factories and offices, but in immortal works of art, — not only in great buildings, but in pictures and music and workmanship in stone and metal, in cotton and wool fabrics. But the British government in India is not personal. It is official and therefore an abstraction. It has nothing to express in the true language of art. For law, efficiency and exploitation cannot sing themselves into epic stones. Lord Lytton, who unfortunately was gifted with more imagination than was necessary for an Indian Viceroy, tried to copy one of the state functions of the Moghals, — the Durbar ceremony. But state ceremonials are works of art. They naturally spring from the reciprocity of personal relationship between the people and their monarch. When they are copies, they show all the signs of the spurious.

How utility and sentiments take different lines in their expression can be seen in the dress of a man compared with that of a woman. A man's dress, as a rule, shuns all that is unnecessary and merely decorative. But a woman has naturally selected the decorative, not only in her dress, but in her manners. She has to be picturesque and musical to make manifest what she truly is, — because, in her position in the world, woman is more concrete and personal than man. She is not to be judged merely by her usefulness, but by her delightfulness. Therefore she takes infinite care in expressing, not her profession, but her personality.

The principal object of art, also, being the expression of personality, and nothing that is abstract and analytical, it necessarily uses the language of picture and music. This has led to a confusion in our thought that the object of art is the production of beauty; whereas, beauty in art has been the mere instrument and not its complete and ultimate significance.

As a consequence of this, we have often heard it argued whether manner, rather than matter, is the essential element in art. Such arguments become endless, like pouring water into a vessel whose bottom has been taken away. These discussions owe their origin to the idea that beauty is the object of art, and, because mere matter cannot have the property of beauty, it becomes a question whether manner is not the principal factor in art.

But the truth is, analytical treatment will not help us in discovering what is the vital point in art. For the true principle of art is the principle of unity. When we want to know the food-value of certain of our diets, we find it in their component parts; but its taste-value is in its unity, which cannot be analyzed. Matter, taken by itself, is an abstraction which can be dealt with by science; also manner, which is merely manner, is an abstraction which comes under the laws of rhetoric. But when they are indissolubly one, then they find their harmonics in our personality, which is an organic complex of matter and manner, thoughts and things, motives and actions.

Therefore we find all abstract ideas are out of place in true art, where, in order to gain admission, they must come under the disguise of personification. This is the reason why poetry tries to select words that have vital qualities, — words that are not for mere information, but have become naturalized in our hearts and have not been worn out of their shapes by too constant use in the market. For instance, the English word "consciousness" has not yet outgrown the cocoon stage of its scholastic inertia, therefore it is seldom used in poetry; whereas its Indian synonym "chetana" is a vital word and is of constant poetical use. On the other hand the English word "feeling" is fluid with life, but its Bengali synonym "anubhuti" is refused in poetry, because it merely has a meaning and no flavour. And likewise there are some truths, coming from science and philosophy, that have acquired life's colour and taste, and some that have not. Until they have done this, they are, for art, like uncooked vegetables, unfit to be served at a feast. History, so long as it copies science and deals with abstractions, remains outside the domain of literature. But, as a narrative of facts, it takes its place by the side of the epic poem. For narration of historical facts imparts to the time to which they belong a taste of personality.

Those periods become human to us, we feel their living heart-beats.

The world and the personal man, — are face to face, as friends who question one another and exchange their inner secrets. The world asks the inner man, — "Friend, have you seen me? Do you love me? — not the one who provides you with foods and fruits, not the one whose laws you have found out, but the one who is personal, individual?"

The artist's answer is "Yes, I have seen you, I have loved and known you, — not that I have any need of you, not that I have taken you and used your laws for my own purposes of power. I know the forces that act and drive and lead to power, but it is not that. I see you, where you are what I am."

But how do you know that the artist has known, has seen, has come face to face with this Personality?

When I first meet any one who is not yet my friend, I observe all the numberless unessential things which attract the attention at first sight:

and in the wilderness of that diversity of facts the friend who is to be my friend is lost.

When our steamer reached the coast of Japan, one of our passengers, a Japanese, was coming back home from Rangoon; we on the other hand were reaching that shore for the first time in our life. There was a great difference in our outlook. We noted every little peculiarity, and innumerable small things occupied our attention. But the Japanese passenger dived at once into the personality, the soul of the land, where his own soul found satisfaction. *He* saw fewer things, *we* saw more things; but what he saw was the soul of Japan. It could not be gauged by any quantity or number, but by something invisible and deep. It could not be said that, because we saw those innumerable things, we saw Japan better, but rather the reverse.

If you ask me to draw some particular tree, and I am no artist, I try to copy every detail, lest I should otherwise lose the peculiarity of the tree, forgetting that the peculiarity is not the personality. But when the true artist comes, he overlooks all details and gets into the essential characterization.

Our rational man also seeks to simplify things into their inner principle; to get rid of the details; to get to the heart of things where things are One. But the difference is this, — the scientist seeks an impersonal principle of unification, which can be applied to all things. For instance he destroys the human body, which is personal, in order to find out physiology, which is impersonal and general.

But the Artist finds out the unique, the individual, which yet is in the heart of the universal. When he looks on a tree, he looks on that tree as unique, not as the botanist who generalizes and classifies. It is the function of the Artist to particularize that one tree. How does he do it? Not through the peculiarity which is the discord of the unique, but through the personality which is harmony. Therefore he has to find out the inner concordance of that one thing with its outer surroundings of all things.

The greatness and beauty of Oriental art, especially in Japan and China, consist in this, that there the artists have seen this soul of things and they believe in it. The West may believe in the soul of Man, but she does not really believe that the universe has a soul. Yet this is the belief of the East, and the whole mental contribution of the East to mankind is filled with this idea. So we, in the East, need not go into details and emphasize them; for the most important thing is this universal soul, for which the Eastern sages have sat in meditation, and Eastern artists have joined them in artistic realization.

Because we have faith in this universal soul, we in the East know that Truth, Power, Beauty, lie in Simplicity, — where it is transparent, where things do not obstruct the inner vision. Therefore, all our sages have tried to make their lives simple and pure, because thus they have the realization of a positive Truth, which, though invisible, is more real than the gross and the numerous.

When we say that art deals only with those truths that are personal, we do not exclude philosophical ideas which are apparently abstract. They are quite common in our Indian literature, because they have been woven with the fibres of our personal nature. I give here an instance which will make my point clear. The following is a translation of an Indian poem written by a woman poet of mediæval India, — its subject is Life.

I salute the Life which is like a sprouting seed,
With its one arm upraised in the air,
and the other down in the soil;
The Life which is one in its outer form and its inner sap;
The Life that ever appears, yet ever eludes
The Life that comes I salute, and the Life that goes;
I salute the Life that is revealed and that is hidden;
I salute the Life in suspense, standing still like a mountain,
And the Life of the surging sea of fire;

The Life that is tender like a lotus, and hard
like a thunderbolt.
I salute the Life which is of the mind, with its
one side in the dark and the other in the
light.
I salute the Life in the house and the Life
abroad in the unknown,
The Life full of joy and the Life weary with its
pains,
The Life eternally moving, rocking the world
into stillness,
The Life deep and silent, breaking out into roar-
ing waves.

This idea of life is not a mere logical deduction; it is as real to the poetess as the air to the bird who feels it at every beat of its wings. Woman has realized the mystery of life in her child more intimately than man has done. This woman's nature in the poet has felt the deep stir of life in all the world. She has known it to be infinite, — not through any reasoning process, but through the illumination of her

AT THE SAN DIEGO EXPOSITION

feeling. Therefore the same idea, which is a mere abstraction to one whose sense of the reality is limited, becomes luminously real to another whose sensibility has a wider range. We have often heard the Indian mind being described by the Western critics as metaphysical, because it is ready to soar in the infinite. But it has to be noted that the infinite is not a mere matter of philosophical speculation to India; it is real to her as the sunlight. She must see it, feel it, make use of it in her life. Therefore it has come out so profusely in her symbolism of worship, in her literature. The poet of the Upanishat has said that the slightest movement of life would be impossible if the sky were not filled with infinite joy. This universal presence was as much of a reality to him as the earth under his feet, nay, even more. The realization of this has broken out in a song of an Indian poet who was born in the fifteenth century:

"There falls the rhythmic beat of life and death:
Rapture wells forth, and all space is radiant
with light.

There the unstruck music is sounded; it is the
love music of three worlds.
There millions of lamps of sun and moon are
burning;
There the drum beats and the lover swings
in play.
There love songs resound, and light rains in
showers."

In India, the greater part of our literature is religious, because God with us is not a distant God; He belongs to our homes, as well as to our temples. We feel His nearness to us in all the human relationship of love and affection, and in our festivities He is the chief guest whom we honour. In seasons of flowers and fruits, in the coming of the rain, in the fulness of the autumn, we see the hem of His mantle and hear His footsteps. We worship Him in all the true objects of our worship and love Him wherever our love is true. In the woman who is good we feel Him, in the man who is true we know Him, in our children He is born again and again, the Eternal Child. Therefore religious songs are our love songs, and our domestic occurrences, such as the birth of a son, or the coming of the daughter from her husband's house to her parents and her departure again, are woven in our literature as a drama whose counterpart is in the divine.

It is thus that the domain of literature has extended into the region which seems hidden in the depth of mystery and made it human and speaking. It is growing, keeping pace with the conquest made by the human personality in the realm of truth. It is growing, not only into history, science and philosophy, but, with our expanding sympathy, into our social consciousness. The classical literature of the ancient time was only peopled by saints and kings and heroes. It threw no light upon men who loved and suffered in obscurity. But as the illumination of man's personality throws its light upon a wider space, penetrating into hidden corners, the world of art also crosses its frontiers and extends its boundaries into unexplored regions. Thus art is signalizing man's conquest of the world by its symbols of beauty, springing up in spots which were barren of all voice and colours. It is supplying man with his banners, under which he marches to fight against the inane and the inert, proving his living claims far and wide in God's creation. Even the spirit of the desert has owned its kinship with him, and the lonely pyramids are there as memorials of the meeting of Nature's silence with the silence of the human spirit. The darkness of the caves has yielded its stillness to man's soul, and in exchange has secretly been crowned with the wreath of art. Bells are ringing in temples, in villages and populous towns to proclaim that the infinite is not a mere emptiness to man. This encroachment of man's personality has no limit, and even the markets and factories of the present age, even the schools where children of man are imprisoned and jails where are the criminals, will be mellowed with the touch of art, and lose their distinction of rigid discordance with life. For the one effort of man's personality is to transform everything with which he has any true concern into the human. And art is like the spread of vegetation, to show how far man has reclaimed the desert for his own.

We have said before that where there is an element of the superfluous in our heart's relationship with the world, Art has its birth. In other words, where our personality feels its wealth it breaks out in display. What we devour for ourselves is totally spent. What overflows our need becomes articulate. The stage of pure utility is like the state of heat which is dark. When it surpasses itself, it becomes white heat and then it is expressive.

Take, for instance, our delight in eating. It is soon exhausted, it gives no indication of the infinite. Therefore, though in its extensiveness it is more universal than any other passion, it is rejected by art. It is like an immigrant coming to these Atlantic shores, who can show no cash balance in his favour.

In our life we have one side which is finite, where we exhaust ourselves at every step, and we have another side, where our aspiration, enjoyment and sacrifice are infinite. This infinite side of man must have its revealments in some symbols which have the elements of immortality. There it naturally seeks perfection. Therefore it refuses all that is flimsy and feeble and incongruous. It builds for its dwelling a paradise, where only those materials are used that have transcended the earth's mortality.

For men are the children of light. Whenever they fully realize themselves they feel their immortality. And, as they feel it, they extend their realm of the immortal into every region of human life.

This building of his true world, — the living world of truth and beauty, — is the function of Art.

Man is true, where he feels his infinity, where he is divine, and the divine is the creator in him. Therefore with the attainment of his truth he creates. For he can truly live in his own creation and make out of God's world his own world. This is the heaven of his own, the heaven of ideas shaped into perfect forms, with which he surrounds himself; where his children are born, where they learn how to live and to die, how to love and to fight, where they know that the real is not that which is merely seen and wealth is not that which is stored. If man could only listen to the voice that rises from the heart of his own creation, he would hear the same message that came from the Indian sage of the ancient time:

"Hearken to me, ye children of the Immortal, dwellers of the heavenly worlds, I have known the supreme Person who comes as light from the dark beyond."

Yes it is that Supreme Person, who has made himself known to man and made this universe so deeply personal to him. Therefore, in India, our places of pilgrimage are there, where in the confluence of the river and the sea, in the eternal snow of the mountain peak, in the lonely sea-shore, some aspect of the infinite is revealed which has its great voice for our heart, and there man has left in his images and temples, in his carvings of stone, these words,—

"Hearken to me, I have known the Supreme Person." In the mere substance and law of this world we do not meet the person, but where the sky is blue, and the grass is green, where the flower has its beauty and fruit its taste, where there is not only perpetuation of race, but joy of living and love of fellow creatures, sympathy and self-sacrifice, there is revealed to us the Person who is infinite. There, not merely facts are pelted down upon our heads, but we feel the bond of the personal relationship binding our hearts with this world through all time. And this is Reality, which is truth made our own, — truth that has its eternal relation with the Supreme Person. This world whose soul seems to be aching for expression in its endless rhythm of lines and colours, music and movements, hints and whispers, and all the suggestion of the inexpressible, finds its harmony in the ceaseless longing of the human heart to make the Person manifest in its own creations.

The desire for the manifestation of this Person

makes us lavish with all our resources. When we accumulate wealth, we have to account for every penny; we reason accurately and we act with care. But when we set about to express our wealthiness, we seem to lose sight of all lines of limit. In fact, none of us has wealth enough fully to express what we mean by wealthiness. When we try to save our life from an enemy's attack, we are cautious in our movements. But when we feel impelled to express our personal bravery, we willingly take risks and go to the length of losing our lives. We are careful of expenditure in our everyday life, but on festive occasions, when we express our joy, we are thriftless even to the extent of going beyond our means. For when we are intensely conscious of our own personality, we are apt to ignore the tyranny of facts. We are temperate in our dealings with the man with whom our relation is the relationship of prudence. But we feel we have not got enough for those whom we love. The poet says of the beloved:

"It seems to me that I have gazed at your beauty from the beginning of my existence, that I have kept you in my arms for countless ages, yet it has not been enough for me."

He says, "Stones would melt in tenderness, if touched by the breeze of your mantle."

He feels that his "eyes long to fly like birds to see his beloved."

Judged from the standpoint of reason these are exaggerations, but from that of the heart, freed from limits of facts, they are true.

Is it not the same in God's creation? There, forces are mere facts and matters are also, — they have their strict accounts kept and they can be accurately weighed and measured. Only beauty is not a mere fact; it cannot be accounted for, it cannot be surveyed and mapped. It is an expression. Facts are like wine cups that carry it, they are hidden by it, it overflows them. It is infinite in its suggestions, it is extravagant in its words. It is personal, therefore, beyond science. It sings as does the poet, "It seems to me that I have gazed at you from the beginning of my existence, that I have kept you in my arms for countless ages, yet it has not been enough for me."

So we find that our world of expression does not accurately coincide with the world of facts, because personality surpasses facts on every side. It is conscious of its infinity and creates from its abundance; and because, in art, things are challenged from the standpoint of the immortal Person, those which are important in our customary life of facts become unreal when placed on the pedestal of art. A newspaper account of some domestic incident in the life of a commercial magnate may create agitation in Society, yet would lose all its proportion if placed by the side of great works of art. We can well imagine how it would hide its face in shame, if by some cruel accident it found itself in the neighbourhood of Keats' "Ode on a Grecian Urn."

Yet the very same incident, when treated deeply, divested of its conventional superficiality, has a better claim in art than the negotiation of raising a big loan for China, or the defeat of British diplomacy in Turkey. A mere household event of a husband's jealousy of his wife, as depicted in one of Shakespeare's tragedies, has greater value in the realm of art than the code of caste regulations in Manu's scripture or the law prohibiting inhabitants of one part of the world from receiving human treatment in another. For when facts are looked upon as mere facts, having their chain of consequences in the world of facts, they are rejected by art.

When, however, such laws and regulations as I have mentioned are viewed in their application to some human individual, in all their injustice, insult and pain, then they are seen in their complete truth and they become subjects for art. The disposition of a great battle may be a great fact, but it is useless for the purpose of art. But what that battle has caused to a single individual soldier, separated from his loved ones and maimed for his life, has a vital value for art which deals with reality.

Man's social world is like some nebulous

system of stars, consisting largely of a mist of abstractions, with such names as society, state, nation, commerce, politics and war. In their dense amorphousness man is hidden and truth is blurred. The one vague idea of war covers a multitude of miseries from our sight, and obscures our sense of reality. The idea of the nation is responsible for crimes that would be appalling, if the mist could be removed for a moment. The idea of society has created forms of slavery without number, which we tolerate simply because it has deadened our consciousness of the reality of the personal man. In the name of religion deeds have been done that would exhaust all the resources of hell itself for punishment, because with its creeds and dogmas it has applied an extensive plaster of anæsthetic over a large surface of feeling humanity. Everywhere in man's world the Supreme Person is suffering from the killing of the human reality by the imposition of the abstract. In our schools the idea of the class hides the reality of the school children; — they become students and not individuals. Therefore it does not hurt us to see children's lives crushed, in their classes, like flowers pressed between book leaves. In government, the bureaucracy deals with generalizations and not with men. And therefore it costs it nothing to indulge in wholesale cruelties. Once we accept as truth such a scientific maxim as "Survival of the Fittest" it immediately transforms the whole world of human personality into a monotonous desert of abstraction, where things become dreadfully simple because robbed of their mystery of life.

In these large tracts of nebulousness Art is creating its stars, — stars that are definite in their forms but infinite in their personality. Art is calling us the "children of the immortal," and proclaiming our right to the dwelling in the heavenly worlds.

What is it in man that asserts its immortality in spite of the obvious fact of death? It is not his physical body or his mental organization. It is that deeper unity, that ultimate mystery in him, which, from the centre of his world, radiates towards its circumference; which is in his body, yet transcends his body; which is in his mind, yet grows beyond his mind; which, through the things belonging to him, expresses something that is not in them; which, while occupying his present, overflows its banks of the past and the future. It is the personality of man, conscious of its inexhaustible abundance; it has the paradox in it that it is more than itself; it is more than as it is seen, as it is known, as it is used. And this consciousness of the infinite, in the personal man, ever strives to make its expressions immortal and to make the whole world its own. In Art the person in us is sending its answers to the Supreme Person, who reveals Himself to us in a world of endless beauty across the lightless world of facts.

THE WORLD OF PERSONALITY

THE WORLD OF PERSONALITY

"THE night is like a dark child just born of her mother day. Millions of stars crowding round its cradle watch it, standing still, afraid lest it should wake up."

I am ready to go on in this strain, but I am interrupted by Science laughing at me. She takes objection to my statement that stars are standing still.

But if it is a mistake, then apology is not due from me but from those stars themselves. It is quite evident that they are standing still. It is a fact that is impossible to argue away.

But science *will* argue, it is her habit. She says, "When you think that stars are still, that only proves that you are too far from them."

I have my answer ready, that when you say that stars are rushing about, it only proves that you are too near them.

Science is astonished at my temerity.

But I obstinately hold my ground and say that if Science has the liberty to take the side of the near and fall foul of the distant, she cannot blame me when I take the opposite side and question the veracity of the near.

Science is emphatically sure that the near view is the most reliable view.

But I doubt whether she is consistent in her opinions. For when I was sure that the earth was flat under my feet, she corrected me by saying that the near view was not the correct view, that to get at the complete truth it is necessary to see it from a distance.

I am willing to agree with her. For do we not know that a too near view of ourselves is the egotistical view, which is the flat and the detached view — but that when we see ourselves in others, we find that the truth about us is round and continuous?

But if Science at all has faith in the wholesomeness of distance then she must give up her superstition about the restlessness of the stars. We the children of the earth attend our night school to have a glimpse of the world as a whole. Our great teacher knows that the complete view of the universe is too awful for our sight, as is that of the midday sun. It is necessary to see it through a smoked glass. Kind Nature has held before our eyes the smoked glass of the night and of the distance. And what do we see through it? We see that the world of stars is still. For we see these stars in their relation to each other, and they appear to us like chains of diamonds hanging on the neck of some god of silence. But Astronomy like a curious child plucks out an individual star from that chain and then we find it rolling about.

The difficulty is to decide whom to trust. The evidence of the world of stars is simple. You have but to raise your eyes and see their face and you believe them. They do not set before you elaborate arguments, and to my mind, that is the surest test of reliability. They do not break their hearts if you refuse to believe them. But when some one of these stars singly comes down from the platform of the universe and slyly whispers its information into the ears of mathematics, we find the whole story different.

Therefore let us boldly declare that both facts are equally true about the stars. Let us say that they are unmoved in the plane of the distant and they are moving in the plane of the near. The stars in their one relation to me are truly still and in their other relation are truly moving. The distant and the near are the keepers of two different sets of facts, but they both belong to one truth which is their master. Therefore when we take the side of the one to revile the other, we hurt the truth which comprehends them both.

About this truth the Indian sage of Ishopanishat says: "It moves. It moves not. It is distant. It is near."

The meaning is, when we follow truth in its parts which are near, we see truth moving. When we know truth as a whole, which is looking at it from a distance, it remains still. As we follow a book in its chapters the book moves, but when we have known the whole book, then we find it standing still, holding all the chapters in their interrelations.

There is a point where in the mystery of existence contradictions meet; where movement is not all movement and stillness is not all stillness; where the idea and the form, the within and the without, are united; where infinite becomes finite, yet not losing its infinity. If this meeting is dissolved, then things become unreal.

When I see a rose leaf through a microscope, I see it in a more extended space than it usually occupies for me. The more I extend the space the more it becomes vague. So that in the pure infinite it is neither rose-leaf nor anything at all. It only becomes a rose-leaf where the infinite reaches finitude at a particular point. When we disturb that point towards the small or the great, the rose-leaf begins to assume unreality.

It is the same with regard to time. If by some magic I could remain in my normal plane of time while enhancing its quickness with regard to the rose leaf, condensing, let us say, a month into a minute, then it would rush through its point of first appearance to that of its final disappearance with such a speed that I would hardly be able to see it. One can be sure that there are things in this world which are known by other creatures, but which, since their time is not synchronous with ours, they are nothing to us. The phenomenon which a dog perceives as a smell does not keep its time with that of our nerves, therefore it falls outside our world.

Let me give an instance. We have heard of prodigies in mathematics who can do difficult sums in an incredibly short time. With regard to mathematical calculations their minds are acting in a different plane of time, not only from ours, but also from their own in other spheres of life. As if the mathematical part of their minds is living in a comet, while the other parts are the inhabitants of this earth. Therefore the process through which their minds rush into their results is not only invisible to us, it is not even seen by themselves.

It is a well-known fact that often our dreams flow in a measure of time different from that of our waking consciousness. The fifty minutes of our sundial of dreamland may be represented by five minutes of our clock. If from the vantage of our wakeful time we could watch these dreams, they would rush past us like an express train. Or if from the window of our swift-flying dreams we could watch the slower world of our waking consciousness, it would seem receding away from us at a great speed. In fact if the thoughts that move in other minds than our own were open to us, our perception of them would be different from theirs, owing to our difference of mental time. If we could adjust our focus of time according to our whims, we would see the waterfall standing still and the pine forest running fast like the waterfall of a green Niagara.

So that it is almost a truism to say that the world is what we perceive it to be. We imagine that our mind is a mirror, that it is more or less accurately reflecting what is happening outside us. On the contrary our mind itself is the principal element of creation. The world, while

I am perceiving it, is being incessantly created for myself in time and space.

The variety of creation is owing to the mind seeing different phenomena in different foci of time and space. When it sees stars in a space which may be metaphorically termed as dense, then they are close to each other and motionless. When it sees planets, it sees them in much less density of sky and then they appear far apart and moving. If we could have the sight to see the molecules of a piece of iron in a greatly different space, they could be seen in movement. But because we see things in various adjustments of time and space therefore iron is iron, water is water, and clouds are clouds for us.

It is a well-known psychological fact that by adjustment of our mental attitude things seem to change their properties, and objects that were pleasurable become painful to us and vice versa. Under a certain state of exultation of mind mortification of the flesh has been resorted to by men to give them pleasure. Instances of extreme martyrdom seem to us superhuman because the mental attitude under the influence of which they become possible, even desirable, has not been experienced by us. In India, cases of fire walking have been observed by many, though they have not been scientifically investigated. There may be differences of opinion about the degree of efficacy of faith cure, showing the influence of mind upon matter, but its truth has been accepted and acted upon by men from the early dawn of history. The methods of our moral training have been based upon the fact that by changing our mental focus, our perspective, the whole world is changed and becomes in certain respects a different creation, with things of changed value. Therefore what is valuable to a man when he is bad becomes worse than valueless when he is good.

Walt Whitman shows a great dexterity in his poems in changing his position of mind and thus changing his world with him from that of other peoples, rearranging the meaning of things in different proportions and forms. Such mobility of mind plays havoc with things whose foundations lie fixed in convention. Therefore he says in one of his poems:

"I hear that it was charged against me that I
sought to destroy institutions;
But really I am neither for nor against institutions;
(What indeed have I in common with them —
Or what with the destruction of them?)
Only I will establish in thee Mannahatta, and in every city of these States, inland and seaboard,
And in the fields and woods, and above every keel, little or large, that dents the water,
Without edifices, or rules, or trustees or any argument,
This institution of dear love of comrades."

Institutions which are so squarely built, so solid and thick become like vapour in this poet's world. It is like a world of Röntgen rays, for which some of the solid things of the world have no existence whatever. On the other hand love of comrades, which is a fluid thing in the ordinary world, which seems like clouds that pass and repass the sky without leaving a trace of a track, is to the poet's world more stable than all institutions. Here he sees things in a time in which the mountains pass away like shadows, but the rainclouds with their seeming transitoriness are eternal. He perceives in his world that this love of comrades, like clouds that require no solid foundation, is stable and true, is established without edifices, rules, trustees or arguments.

When the mind of a person like Walt Whitman moves in a time different from that of others, his world does not necessarily come to ruin through dislocation, because there in the centre of his world dwells his own personality. All the facts and shapes of this world are related to this central creative power, therefore they become interrelated spontaneously. His world may be like a comet among stars, different in its movements from others, but it has its own consistency because of the central personal force. It may be a bold world or even a mad world, with an immense orbit swept by its eccentric tail, yet it is a world.

But with science it is different. For she tries to do away altogether with that central personality, in relation to which the world is a world. Science sets up an impersonal and unalterable standard of space and time which is not the standard of creation. Therefore at its fatal touch the reality of the world is so hopelessly disturbed that it vanishes in an abstraction where things become nothing at all. For the world is not atoms and molecules or radio-activity or other forces, the diamond is not carbon, and light is not vibrations of ether. You can never come to the reality of creation by contemplating it from the point of view of destruction. Not only the world but God himself is divested of reality by Science, which subjects him to analysis in the laboratory of reason outside our personal relationship and then describes the result as unknown and unknowable. It is a mere tautology to say that God is unknowable, when we leave altogether out of account the person who can and who does know him. It is the same thing as saying that food is uneatable when the eater is absent. Our dry moralists also play the same tricks with us in order to wean away our hearts from their desired objects. Instead of creating for us a world in which moral ideals find their natural places in beauty they begin to wreck the world that we have built ourselves, however imperfectly. They put moral maxims in the place of human personality and give us the view of things in their dissolution to prove that behind their appearances they are hideous deceptions. But when you deprive truth of its appearance, it loses the best part of its reality. For appearance is a personal relationship; it is for me. Of this appearance, which seems to be of the surface, but which carries the message of the inner spirit, your poet has said:

"Beginning my studies, the first step pleased me so much,
The mere fact, consciousness — these forms — the power of motion
The least insect or animal — the senses — eyesight — love;

The first step, I say, aw'd me and pleased me so much,
I have hardly gone, and hardly wished to go, any farther,
But stop and loiter all the time, and sing it in ecstatic songs."

Our scientific world is our world of reasoning. It has its greatness and uses and attractions. We are ready to pay the homage due to it. But when it claims to have discovered the real world for us and laughs at the worlds of all simple-minded men, then we must say it is like a general grown intoxicated of his power, usurping the throne of his king. For the reality of the world belongs to the personality of man and not to reasoning, which is useful and great but which is not the man himself.

If we could fully know what a piece of music was in Beethoven's mind, we could ourselves become so many Beethovens. But because we cannot grasp its mystery, we may altogether distrust the element of Beethoven's personality in his Sonata—though we are fully aware that its true value lies in its power of touching the depth of our own personality. But it is simpler to keep observation of the facts when that sonata is played upon the piano. We can count the black and white keys of the keyboard, measure the relative lengths of the strings, the strength, velocity and order of sequence in the movements of fingers and triumphantly assert that this is Beethoven's Sonata. Not only so, we can predict the accurate production of the same sonata wherever and whenever our experiment is repeated according to those observations. By constantly dealing with the sonata from this point of view we may forget that both in its origin and object dwell the personality of man, and however accurate and orderly may be the facts of the interactions of the fingers and strings they do not comprehend the ultimate reality of the music.

A game is a game where there is a player to play it. Of course, there is a law of the game which it is of use to us to analyze and to master.

But if it be asserted that in this law is its reality, then we cannot accept it. For the game is what it is to the players. The game changes its aspects according to the personality of its players: for some its end is the lust of gain, in others that of applause; some find in it the means for whiling away time and some the means for satisfying their social instinct, and there are others who approach it in the spirit of disinterested curiosity for studying its secrets. Yet all through its manifold aspects its law remains the same. For the nature of Reality is the variedness of its unity. And the world is like this game to us — it is the same and yet it is not the same to us all.

Science deals with this element of sameness, the law of perspective and colour combination, and not with the pictures — the pictures which are the creations of a personality and which appeal to the personality of those who see them. Science does it by eliminating from its field of research the personality of creation and fixing its attention only upon the medium of creation.

SIR RABINDRANATH TAGORE AND W. W. PEARSON AT RIVERSIDE, CALIFORNIA

What is this medium? It is the medium of finitude which the Infinite Being sets before him for the purpose of his self-expression. It is the medium which represents his self-imposed limitations — the law of space and time, of form and movement. This law is Reason, which is universal — Reason which guides the endless rhythm of the creative idea, perpetually manifesting itself in its ever changing forms.

Our individual minds are the strings which catch the rhythmic vibrations of this universal mind and respond in music of space and time. The quality and number and pitch of our mind strings differ and their tuning has not yet come to its perfection, but their law is the law of the universal mind which is the instrument of finitude upon which the Eternal Player plays his dance music of creation.

Because of the mind instruments which we possess we also have found our place as creators. We create not only art and social organizations, but our inner nature and outer surroundings, the truth of which depends upon their harmony with the law of the universal mind. Of course, our creations are mere variations upon God's great theme of the universe. When we produce discords, they either have to end in a harmony or in silence. Our freedom as a creator finds its highest joy in contributing its own voice in the concert of the world-music.

Science is apprehensive of the poet's sanity. She refuses to accept the paradox of the infinite assuming finitude.

I have nothing to say in my defence except that this paradox is much older than I am. It is the paradox that is at the root of existence. It is as mysterious yet as simple as the fact that I am aware of this wall which is a miracle that can never be explained.

Let me go back to the sage of Ishopanishat and hear what he says about the contradiction of the infinite and the finite. He says:

"They enter the region of the dark who are solely occupied with the knowledge of the finite, and they into a still greater darkness who are solely occupied with the knowledge of the infinite."

Those who pursue the knowledge of finite for its own sake cannot find truth. For it is a dead wall obstructing the beyond. This knowledge merely accumulates but does not illuminate. It is like a lamp without its light, a violin without its music. You cannot know a book by measuring and weighing and counting its pages, by analyzing its paper. An inquisitive mouse may gnaw through the wooden frame of a piano, may cut all its strings to pieces and yet travel farther and farther away from the music. This is the pursuit of the finite for its own sake.

But according to the Upanishat the sole pursuit of the infinite leads to a deeper darkness. For the absolute infinite is emptiness. The finite is something. It may be a mere cheque-book with no account in the bank. But the absolute infinite has no cash and not even a cheque-book. Profound may be the mental darkness of the primitive man who lives in the conviction that each individual apple falls to the ground according to some individual caprice, but it is nothing compared to the blindness of him who lives in the meditation of the law of gravitation which has no apple or anything else that falls.

Therefore Ishopanishat in the following verse says:

"He who knows that the knowledge of the finite and the infinite is combined in one, crosses death by the help of the knowledge of the finite and achieves immortality by the help of the knowledge of the infinite."

The infinite and the finite are one as song and singing. The singing is incomplete; by a continual process of death it gives up the song which is complete. The absolute infinite is like a music which is devoid of all definite tunes and therefore meaningless.

The absolute eternal is timelessness, and that has no meaning at all,—it is merely a word. The reality of the eternal is there, where it contains all times in itself.

Therefore Upanishat says: "They enter the region of darkness who pursue the transitory. But they enter the region of still greater darkness who pursue the eternal. He who knows the transitory and the eternal combined together crosses the steps of death by the help of the transitory and reaches immortality by the help of the eternal."

We have seen that forms of things and their changes have no absolute reality at all. Their truth dwells in our personality, and only there it is real and not abstract. We have seen that a mountain and a waterfall would become something else, or nothing at all to us, if our movement of mind changed in time and space.

We have also seen that this relational world of ours is not arbitrary. It is individual, yet it is universal. My world is mine, its element is my mind, yet is not wholly unlike your world. Therefore it is not in my own individual personality that this reality is contained, but in an infinite personality.

When in its place we substitute law, then the whole world crumbles into abstractions; then it is elements and force, eons and electrons; it loses its appearance, its touch and taste; the world drama with its language of beauty is hushed, the music is silent, the stage mechanism becomes a ghost of itself in the dark, an unimaginable shadow of nothing, standing before no spectator.

In this connection I quote once again your poet-seer, Walt Whitman:

"When I heard the learned astronomer,
When the proofs, the figures, were ranged in columns before me,
When I was shown the charts and diagrams, to add, divide and measure them,
When I sitting heard the astronomer where he lectured with much applause in the lecture room,
How soon unaccountably I became tired and sick,
Till rising and gliding out I wandered off by myself,
In the mystical moist night-air, and from time to time,
Looked up in perfect silence at the stars."

The prosody of the stars can be explained in the class room by diagrams, but the poetry of the stars is in the silent meeting of soul with soul, at the confluence of the light and the dark, where the infinite prints its kiss on the forehead of the finite, where we can hear the music of the Great I AM peeling from the grand organ of creation through its countless reeds in endless harmony. It is perfectly evident that the world is movement. (The Sanskrit word for the world means "the moving one.") All its forms are transitory, but that is merely its negative side. All through its changes it has a chain of relationship which is eternal. In a story-book the sentences run on, but the positive element of the book is the relation of the sentences in the story. This relation reveals a will of personality in its author which establishes its harmony with the personality of the reader. If the book were a collection of disjointed words of no movement and meaning, then we would be justified in saying that it was a product of chance and then it would have no response from the personality of the reader. In the like manner all through its changes the world is not a mere runaway evasion to us, and because of its movements it reveals to us something which is eternal.

For revealment of idea, form is absolutely necessary. But the idea which is infinite cannot be expressed in forms which are absolutely finite. Therefore forms must always move and change, they must necessarily die to reveal the deathless. The expression as expression has to be definite, which can only be in its form; but at the same time, as the expression of the infinite, it has to be indefinite, which can only be in its movement. Therefore when the world takes its shape it always transcends its shape; it carelessly runs out of itself to say that its meaning is more than what it can contain.

The moralist sadly shakes his head and says that this world is vanity. But that vanity is not vacuity — truth is in that vainness itself. If the world remained still and became final, then it would be a prison house of orphaned facts that had lost their freedom of truth, the truth that is infinite. Therefore what the modern thinker says is true in this sense, that in movement lies the meaning of all things—because the meaning does not entirely rest in the things themselves but in that which is indicated by their outgrowing of their limits. This is what Isha Upanishat means when it says that neither the transitory nor the eternal has any meaning separately. When they are known in harmony with each other, only then through its own help we cross the transitory and realize the immortal.

Because this world is the world of infinite personality it is the object of our life to establish a perfect and personal relationship with it, is the teaching of Isha Upanishat. Therefore it begins with the following verse:

Know that all that moves in this moving world is held by the infinity of God; and enjoy by that which he renounces. Desire not after other possessions.

That is to say, we have to know that these world movements are not mere blind movements, they are related to the will of a Supreme Person. But a mere knowledge of truth is imperfect because impersonal. But enjoyment is personal and the God of my enjoyment moves; he is active; he is giving himself. In this act of giving the infinite has taken the aspect of the finite, therefore become real, and there I can have my joy in him.

In our crucible of reason the world of appearance vanishes and we call it illusion. This is the negative view. But our enjoyment is positive. A flower is nothing when we analyze it, but it is positively a flower when we enjoy it. This joy is real because it is personal. And perfect truth is only known perfectly by our personality.

And therefore Upanishat has said: Mind comes back baffled and words also. But he who realizes the joy of Brahma fears nothing.

The following is the translation of another verse in which Ishopanishat deals with the passive and the active aspects of the infinite:

"He who is without a stain, without a body, and therefore without bodily injury or bodily organs of strength, without mixture and without any touch of evil enters into everywhere. He who is the poet, the ruler of mind, the all-becoming, the self-born, dispenses perfect fulfilment to the endless years."

Brahma, in his negative qualities, is quiescent. Brahma, in his positive qualities, acts upon all time. He is the poet, he uses mind as his instrument, he reveals himself in limits, the revelation which comes out of his abundance of joy and not from any outside necessity. Therefore it is he who can fulfil our needs through endless years by giving himself.

From this we find our ideal. Perpetual giving up is the truth of life. The perfection of this is our life's perfection. We are to make this life our poem in all its expressions; it must be fully suggestive of our soul which is infinite, not merely of our possessions which have no meaning in themselves. The consciousness of the infinite in us proves itself by our joy in giving ourselves out of our abundance. And then our work is the process of our renunciation, it is one with our life. It is like the flowing of the river, which is the river itself.

Let us live. Let us have the true joy of life,

which is the joy of the poet in pouring himself out in his poem. Let us express our infinity in everything round us, in works we do, in things we use, in men with whom we deal, in the enjoyment of the world with which we are surrounded. Let our soul permeate our surroundings and create itself in all things, and show its fulness by fulfilling needs of all times. This life of ours has been filled with the gifts of the divine giver. The stars have sung to it, it has been blessed with the daily blessing of the morning light, the fruits have been sweet to it, and the earth has spread its carpet of grass so that it may have its rest. And let it like an instrument fully break out in music of its soul in response to the touch of the infinite soul.

And this is why the poet of the Ishopanishat says:

Doing work in this world thou shouldst wish to live a hundred years. Thus it is with thee and not otherwise. Let not the work of man cling to him.

Only by living life fully can you outgrow it.

When the fruit has served its full term, drawing its juice from the branch, dancing with the wind and maturing in the sun, then it feels in its core the call of the beyond and becomes ready for its career of a wider life. But the wisdom of living is in that which gives you the power to give it up. For death is the gate of immortality. Therefore it is said, Do your work, but let not your work cling to you. For the work expresses your life so long as it flows with it, but when it clings, then it impedes, then it shows, not the life, but itself. Then like the sands carried by the stream it chokes the soul-current. Activity of limbs is in the nature of physical life; but when limbs move in convulsion, then the movements are not in harmony with life, and then they are a disease, like works that cling to a man and kill his soul.

No, we must not slay our souls. We must not forget that life is here to express the eternal in us. If we smother our consciousness of the infinite either by slothfulness or by passionate pursuit of things that have no freedom of greatness in them, then like the fruit whose seed has become dead we go back into the primal gloom of the realm of the unformed. Life is perpetual creation; it has its truth when it outgrows itself in the infinite. But when it stops and accumulates and turns back to itself, when it has lost its outlook upon the beyond, then it must die. Then it is dismissed from the world of growth and with all its heaps of belongings crumbles into the dust of dissolution. Of them Isha Upanishat has said, "Those who slay their souls pass from hence to the gloom of the sunless world."

The question, "What is this soul?" has thus been answered by the Isha Upanishat:

It is one, and though unmoving is swifter than mind; organs of sense cannot reach it; while standing it progresses beyond others that run; in it the life inspiration maintains the fluid forces of life.

The mind has its limitations, the sense organs are severally occupied with things that are before them, but there is a spirit of oneness in us which goes beyond the thoughts of its mind, the movements of its bodily organs, which carries whole eternity in its present moment, because of whose presence the life inspiration ever urges the life forces onward. Because we are conscious of this One in us which is more than all its belongings, which outlives the death of its moments, we cannot believe that it can die. Because it is one, because it is more than its parts, because it is continual survival, perpetual overflow, we feel it beyond all boundaries of death.

This consciousness of oneness beyond all boundaries is the consciousness of soul. And of this soul Isha Upanishat has said: It moves. It moves not. It is in the distant. It is in the near. It is within all. It is outside all.

This is knowing the soul across the boundaries of the near and the distant, of the within and the without. I have known this wonder of wonders, this one in myself which is the centre of all reality for me. But I cannot stop here. I cannot say that it exceeds all boundaries, yet it is bounded by myself. Therefore Isha Upanishat says:

"He who sees all things in the soul and the soul in all things is nevermore hidden."

We are hidden in ourselves, like a truth hidden in isolated facts. When we know that this One in us is One in all, then our truth is revealed.

But this knowledge of the unity of soul must not be an abstraction. It is not that negative kind of universalism which belongs neither to one nor to another. It is not an abstract soul, but it is my own soul which I must realize in others. I must know that if my soul were singularly mine, then it could not be true, at the same time if it were not intimately mine, it would not be real.

Through the help of logic we never could have arrived at the truth that the soul which is the unifying principle in me finds its perfection in its unity in others. We have known it through the joy of this truth. Our delight is in realizing ourselves outside us. When I love, in other words, when I feel I am truer in some one else than myself, then I am glad, for the One in me realizes its truth of unity by uniting with others and there is its joy.

Therefore the spirit of One in God must have the

many for the realization of the unity. And God is giving himself in love to all. Isha Upanishat says, "Thou shouldst enjoy what God is renouncing." He is renouncing; and I have my joy when I feel that he is renouncing himself. For this joy of mine is the joy of love which comes of the renouncing of myself in him.

Where Isha Upanishat teaches us to enjoy God's renunciation it says, Desire not after other man's possessions.

For desire is hindrance to love. It is the movement towards the opposite direction of truth, towards the illusion that self is our final object.

Therefore the realization of our soul has its moral side and its spiritual. The moral side represents training of unselfishness, control of desire; the spiritual side represents sympathy and love. They should be taken together and never separated. The cultivation of the merely moral side of our nature leads us to the dark region of narrowness and hardness of heart, to the intolerant arrogance of goodness; and the cultivation of the merely spiritual side of nature leads us to a still darker region of revelry in intemperance of imagination.

By following the poet of Isha Upanishat we have come to the meaning of all reality, where the infinite is giving himself out through finitude. Reality is the expression of personality, like a poem, like a work of art. The Supreme Being is giving himself in his world and I am making it mine, like a poem which I realize by finding myself in it. If my own personality leaves the centre of my world, then in a moment it loses all its attributes. From this I know that my world exists in relation to me, and I know that it has been given to the personal *me* by a personal being. The process of the giving can be classified and generalized by science, but not the gift. For the gift is the soul unto the soul, therefore it can only be realized by the soul in joy, not analyzed by the reason in logic.

Therefore the one cry of the personal man has been to know the Supreme Person. From the beginning of his history man has been feeling the touch of personality in all creation, and trying to give it names and forms, weaving it in legends round his life and the life of his races, offering it worship and establishing relations with it through countless forms of ceremonials. This feeling of the touch of personality has given the centrifugal impulse in man's heart to break out in a ceaseless flow of reaction, in songs and pictures and poems, in images and temples and festivities. This has been the centripetal force which attracted men into groups and clans and communal organizations. And while man tills his soil and spins his cloths, mates and rears his children, toils for wealth and fights for power he does not forget to proclaim in languages of solemn rhythm, in mysterious symbols, in structures of majestic stone that in the heart of his world he has met the Immortal Person. In the sorrow of death, and suffering of despair, when trust has been betrayed and love desecrated, when existence becomes tasteless and unmeaning, man standing upon the ruins of his hopes stretches his hands to the heavens to feel the touch of the Person across his darkened world.

Man has also known direct communication of the person with the Person, not through the world of forms and changes, the world of extension in time and space, but in the innermost solitude of consciousness, in the region of the profound and the intense. Through this meeting he has felt a creation of a new world, a world of light and love that has no language but of mûsic of silence.

Of this the poet has sung:

"There is an endless world, O my Brother.
And there is a nameless Being of whom nought can be said.
Only he knows who has reached that region:
It is other than all that is heard and said.
No form, no body, no length, no breadth, is seen there:
How can I tell you that which it is?
Kabir says: 'It cannot be told by the words of the mouth, it cannot be written on paper:
It is like a dumb person who tastes a sweet thing — how shall it be explained.'"

No, it cannot be explained, it has to be realized; and when man has done so, he sings:

"The inward and the outward has become as one
sky,
The infinite and the finite are united:
I am drunken with the sight of this All."

The poet in this has reached Reality which is ineffable, where all contradictions have been harmonized. For the ultimate reality is in the Person and not in the law and substance. And man must feel that if this universe is not the manifestation of a Supreme Person, then it is a stupendous deception and a perpetual insult to him. He should know that under such enormous weight of estrangement his own personality would have been crushed out of its shape in the very beginning and have vanished in the meaninglessness of an abstraction that had not even the basis of a mind for its conception.

The poet of Isha Upanishat at the end of his teachings suddenly breaks out in a verse which in the depth of its simplicity carries the lyrical silence of the wide earth gazing at the morning sun. He sings:

"In the golden vessel is hidden the face of truth. O thou Giver of Nourishment, remove the cover for our sight, for us who must know the law of truth. O thou giver of nourishment, thou who movest alone, who dost regulate the creation, who art the spirit of the lord of all creatures, collect thy rays, draw together thy light, let me behold in thee the most blessed of all forms,— the Person who is there, who is there, he is I Am."

Then at the conclusion this poet of deathless personality thus sings of death:

"Life breath is the breath of immortality. The body ends in ashes. O my will, remember thy deeds, O my will, remember thy deeds. O God, O Fire, thou knowest all deeds. Lead us through good path to fulfilment. Separate from us the crooked sin. To thee we offer our speech of salutation."

Here stops the poet of Isha Upanishat, having travelled from life to death and from death to life again; who has had the boldness to see Brahma as the infinite Being and the finite Becoming at the same moment; who declares that life is through work, the work that expresses the soul; whose teaching is to realize our soul in the Supreme Being through our renunciation of self and union with all.

The profound truth to which the poet of Isha Upanishat has given expression is the truth of the simple mind which is in deep love with the mystery of reality and cannot believe in the finality of that logic which by its method of decomposition brings the universe to the brink of dissolution.

Have I not known the sunshine to grow brighter and the moonlight deeper in its tenderness when my heart was filled with a sudden access of love assuring me that this world is one with my soul? When I have sung the coming of the clouds, the pattering of rains has found its pathos in my songs. From the dawn of our history the poets and artists have been infusing the colours and music of their soul into the structure of existence. And from this I have known certainly that the earth and the sky are woven with the fibres of man's mind, which is the universal mind at the same time. If this were not true, then poetry would be false and music a delusion, and the mute world would compel man's heart into utter silence. The Great Master plays; the breath is his own, but the instrument is our mind through which he brings out his songs of creation, and therefore I know that I am not a mere stranger resting in the wayside inn of this earth on my voyage of existence, but I live in a world whose life is bound up with mine. The poet has known that the reality of this world is personal and has sung:

The earth is His joy: His joy is the sky;
His joy is the flashing of the sun and the moon;
His joy is the beginning, the middle, and the end;
His joy is eyes, darkness and light.
Oceans and waves are His joy;
His joy the Saraswati, the Jumana and the
    Ganges.
The Master is One: and life and death,
Union and separation, are all His plays of joy.

THE SECOND BIRTH

THE SECOND BIRTH

For us, inanimate nature is the outside view of existence. We only know how it appears to us, but we do not know what it is. For that we can only know by sympathy.

But the curtain rises, life appears on the stage, and the drama begins whose meaning we come to understand through gestures and language resembling our own. We know what life is, not by outward features, not by analysis of its parts, but by a more immediate perception through sympathy. And this is real knowledge.

We see a tree. It is separate from its surroundings by the fact of its individual life. All its struggle is to keep this separateness of its creative individuality distinct from everything else in the universe. Its life is based upon a dualism, — on one side this individuality of the tree, and on the other the universe.

But if it were a dualism of hostility and mutual

exclusion, then the tree would have no chance to maintain its existence. The whole league of giant forces would pull it to pieces. It is a dualism of relationship. The more perfect the harmony with its world of the sun and the soil and the seasons, the more perfect becomes the tree in its individuality. It is an evil for it when this inter-relation is checked. Therefore life, on its negative side, has to maintain separateness from all else, while, on its positive side, it maintains unity with the universe. In this unity is its fulfilment.

In the life of an animal on its negative side this element of separateness is still more pronounced, and on that account on its positive side its relationship with the world is still wider. Its food is more fully separated from it than that of the tree. It has to seek it and know it under the stimuli of pleasure and pain. Therefore it has a fuller relationship with its world of knowledge and feeling. The same is also true in its case with regard to the separation of sex. These separations, and the consequent efforts after unity, have the effect of heightening the consciousness of self in animals, making their personality richer by their contact with unforeseen obstacles and unexpected possibilities. In the trees the separation from their progeny ends in complete detachment, whereas in animals it leads to a further relationship. Thus the vital interest of animals is still more enlarged in its scope and intensity, and their consciousness is spread over a larger area. This wider kingdom of their individuality they have constantly to maintain through a complex relationship with their world. All obstacles to this are evils.

In man, this dualism of physical life is still more varied. His needs are not only greater in number and therefore requiring larger field for search, but also more complex, requiring deeper knowledge of things. This gives him a greater consciousness of himself. It is his mind which more fully takes the place of the automatic movements and instinctive activities of trees and animals. This mind also has its negative and positive aspects of separateness and unity. For, on the one hand, it separates the objects of knowledge from their knower, and then again unites them in a relationship of knowledge. To the vital relationship of this world of food and sex is added the secondary relation which is mental. Thus we make this world doubly our own by living in it and by knowing it.

But there is another division in man, which is not explained by the character of his physical life. It is the dualism in his consciousness of what is and what ought to be. In the animal this is lacking, its conflict is between what *is* and what is desired; whereas, in man, the conflict is between what *is* desired and what *should be* desired. What is desired dwells in the heart of the natural life, which we share with animals; but what should be desired belongs to a life which is far beyond it.

So, in man, a second birth has taken place. He still retains a good many habits and instincts of his animal life; yet his true life is in the region of what ought to be. In this, though there is a continuation, yet there is also a conflict. Many things that are good for the one life are evil for the other. This necessity of a fight with himself has introduced an element into man's personality which is character. From the life of desire it guides man to the life of purpose. This life is the life of the moral world.

In this moral world we come from the world of nature into the world of humanity. We live and move and have our being in the universal man. A human infant is born into the material universe and into the universe of man at the same time. This latter is a world of ideas and institutions, of stored knowledge and trained habits. It has been built by strenuous endeavours of ages, by martyrdoms of heroic men. Its strata are deposits of the renunciations of countless individuals in all ages and countries. It has its good and evil elements, — the inequalities of its surface and its temperature making the flow of life full of surprises.

This is the world of man's second birth, the extra-natural world, where the dualism of the animal life and the moral makes us conscious of our personality as man. Whatever hinders this life of man from establishing perfect relationship with its moral world is an evil. It is death, — a far greater death than the death of the natural life.

In the natural world, with the help of science, man is turning the forces of matter from tyranny into obedience.

But in his moral world he has a harder task to accomplish. He has to turn his own passions and desires from tyranny into obedience. And continual efforts have been directed towards this end in all times and climates. Nearly all our institutions are the outcome of these endeavours. They are giving directions to our will and digging channels for it in order to allow its course to run easily without useless waste of power.

We have seen that the physical life had its gradual expansion into the mental. The mind of animals is fully engrossed in the search for and knowledge of the immediate necessities of life. In man's case these objects were more varied and therefore a greater mind power was requisite.

AT SANTA BARBARA, CALIFORNIA

Thus we became aware that our world of present needs is one with a world that infinitely transcends our present needs. We came to know that this world not only provides us with food, but with thoughts in a greater measure; that there is a subtle relationship of all things with our mind.

What the intellect is in the world of Nature our will is in the moral world. The more it is freed and widened, the more our moral relationship becomes true, varied and large. Its outer freedom is the freedom from the guidance of pleasure and pain, its inner freedom is from the narrowness of self-desire. We know that when intellect is freed from the bondage of interest it discovers the world of universal reason, with which we must be in harmony fully to satisfy our needs; in the same manner when will is freed from its limitations, when it becomes good, that is to say, when its scope is extended to all men and all time, it discerns a world transcending the moral world of humanity. It finds a world where all our disciplines of moral life find their ultimate truth, and our mind is roused to the idea that there is an infinite medium of truth through which goodness finds its meaning. That I become more in my union with others is not a simple fact of arithmetic. We have known that when different personalities combine in love, which is the complete union, then it is not like adding to the horse power of efficiency, but it is what was imperfect finding its perfection in truth, and therefore in joy; what was meaningless, when unrelated, finding its full meaning in relationship. This perfection is not a thing of measurement or analysis, it is a whole which transcends all its parts. It leads us into a mystery, which is in the heart of things, yet beyond it, — like the beauty of a flower which is infinitely more than its botanical facts; like the sense of humanity itself which cannot be contained in mere gregariousness.

This feeling of perfection in love, which is the feeling of the perfect oneness, opens for us the gate of the world of the Infinite One, who is revealed in the unity of all personalities; who gives truth to sacrifice of self, to death which leads to a larger life, and to loss which leads to a greater gain; who turns the emptiness of renunciation into fulfilment by his own fulness. Here we come to the realm of the greatest division in us, — the division of the finite and the infinite. In this we become conscious of the relationship between what is in us and what is beyond us; between what is in the moment and what is ever to come.

The consciousness of relationship dawned in us with our physical existence, where there was separation and meeting between our individual life and the universal world of things; it took a deeper hue in our mental life, where there was a separation and continual reunion between our individual mind and the universal world of reason; it widened where there was a separation and combination between the individual will and the universal world of human personalities; it came to its ultimate meaning where there was the separation and harmony between the individual One in us and the universal One in infinity. And at this point of the everlasting parting and meeting of the One with the One breaks out the wonderful song of man —

> "That is the Supreme Path of This,
> That is the Supreme Treasure of This,
> That is the Supreme World of This,
> That is the Supreme Joy of This." [1]

Life is the relationship of the That and the This. In the world of things and men, this rhythm of That and This flows on in countless channels of metres; but the meaning of it is absent, till the realization is made perfect in the Supreme That and This.

The relation of the unborn child to its surroundings in the mother's womb is intimate, but there its final meaning is missing. There its wants are ministered to in all their details, but its greatest want remains unfulfilled. It must be born into the world of light and space and free-

[1] Eshāsya paramā gatih,
Eshāsya paramā sampat,
Esho'sya paramo lokah,
Esho'sya parama ānandah.

dom of action. That world is so entirely different in every respect from that of the mother's womb, that, if the unborn child had the power to think, it could never imagine what that wider world was. Yet it has limbs, which have their only meaning in the freedom of the air and light.

In the same manner in the natural world man has all the preparations for the nourishment of his self. There his self is his principal concern, — the self which is detached in its interests from other selves. As is his self, so are the things of his world; they have no other connection in themselves than that of his use. But some faculties grow in him, like the limbs in the unborn child, which give him the power to realize the unity of the world, — the unity which is the property of soul, and not of things. He has the faculty of taking joy in others, in beauty and love, more so than the joy in himself, — the faculty which makes him spurn pleasure and accept pain and death, makes him refuse to acknowledge any limit to his progress, and leads him towards knowledge and action that are of no apparent use to him. This causes conflict with the laws of the natural world, and the principle of the survival of the fittest changes its meaning.

Here comes the greatest suffering of the dualism in man, — dualism of the world of nature and the world of soul. The evil which hurts the natural man is pain, but that which hurts his soul has been given a special name, — it is sin. For it may not be at all realized in pain, yet it is evil, just as blindness or lameness is of no consequence to the embryo, yet becomes a great evil if it continues after birth, for it hinders life's ultimate purpose. Crime is against man, sin is against the divine in us.

What is this divine? It is that which has its right and true meaning in the infinite, which does not believe in the embryonic life of self as the ultimate truth. The travail of birth is upon all humanity — its history is the history of suffering such as no animal can ever realize. All its energies are urging it forward; it has no rest. When it goes to sleep upon its prosperity, binds its life in codes of convention, begins to scoff at its ideals, and wants to withdraw all its forces towards the augmentation of self, then it shows signs of death; its very power becomes the power of destruction, — the power which makes huge preparations for death, not believing in the immortal life.

For all other creatures nature is final. To live, to propagate their race and to die is their end. And they are content. They never cry for salvation, for emancipation from the limits of life; they never feel stifled for breath and knock with all their forces against the boundary walls of their world; they never know what it is to renounce their life of plenty and through privations to seek entrance into the realm of blessedness. They are not ashamed of their desires, they are pure in their appetites; for these belong to their complete life. They are not cruel in their cruelties, not greedy in their greeds; for these end in their objects, which are final in themselves. But man has a further life, and therefore those passions are despised by him which do not acknowledge his infinity.

In man, the life of the animal has taken a further bend. He has come to the beginning of a world, which has to be created by his own will and power. The receptive stage is past, in which the self tries to draw all surrounding things towards its own centre and gives nothing. Man is now upon his career of creative life; he is to give from his abundance. By his incessant movement of renunciation he is to grow. Whatever checks that freedom of endless growth is sin, which is the evil that works against man's eternity. This creative energy in man has shown itself from the beginning of his chapter of life. Even his physical needs are not supplied to him ready-made in nature's nursery. From his primitive days he has been busy creating a world of his own resources from the raw materials that lie around him. Even the dishes of his food are his own creation and, unlike animals, he is born naked and has to create his own clothes. This proves that man has been born from the world of nature's purpose to the world of freedom.

For creation is freedom. It is a prison, to have to live in what is; for it is living in what is not ourselves. There we helplessly allow nature to choose us and choose for us, and thus we come under the law of natural selection. But in our creation we live in what is ours, and there more and more the world becomes a world of our own selection; it moves with our movement and gives way to us according to the turn we take. Thus we find that man is not content with the world that is given to him; he is bent upon making it his own world. And he is taking to pieces the mechanism of the universe to study it and to refit it according to his own requirements. He is restless under the restrictions of nature's arrangements of things. These impede the freedom of his course at every step, and he has to tolerate the tyranny of matter, which his nature refuses to believe final and inevitable.

Even in his savage days he would change things by magical powers. He dreamed, as no animal ever does, of Aladdin's lamp and of the obedient forces of genii to turn the world upside down as it suited him, because his free spirit, in its movements, stumbled against things arranged without consideration for him. He was obliged to behave as if he must follow the arrangement of nature, which had not his consent, or die. But this, in spite of hard facts against him, he never could believe in his heart of hearts. Therefore he dreamed of the paradise where he could be free, of the fairy land, of the epic age when man had constant coöperation with gods, of the philosopher's stone, of the elixir of life. Though he saw no gate opening out anywhere, he groped for it, he fretted, he desired and prayed for an entrance to freedom with all his might. For instinctively he felt that this world was not his final world, and unless he had another world his soul was a meaningless torment to him.

Science guides man's rebellion of freedom against Nature's rule. She is working to give into man's hand Nature's magic wand of power; she is to free our spirit from the slavery of things. Science has a materialistic appearance, because she is engaged in breaking the prison of matter and working in the rubbish heap of the ruins. At the invasion of a new country plunder becomes the rule of the day. But when that country is conquered, things become different, and those who robbed act as policemen to restore peace and security. Science is at the beginning of the invasion of the material world and there goes on a furious scramble for plunder. Often things look hideously materialistic, shamelessly belying man's own nature. But the day will come when some of the great powers of nature will be at the beck and call of every individual, and at least the prime necessities of life will be supplied to all with very little care and cost. To live will be as easy to man as to breathe, and his spirit will be free to create his own world.

In early days, when science had not found the keys to nature's storehouses of power, man still had the courage of stoicism to defy matter. He said he could go without food, and clothes were not absolutely necessary for him to save him from extremes of temperature. He loved to take pride in mortifying the flesh. It was his pleasure openly to proclaim that he paid very few of the taxes which nature claimed from him. He proved that he utterly disdained the fear of pain and death, with the help of which nature exacted servitude from him.

Why was this pride? Why has man always chafed against the humiliation of bending his neck to physical necessities? Why could he never reconcile himself to accept the limitations of nature as absolute? Why could he, in his physical and moral world, attempt impossibilities that stagger imagination, and, in spite of repeated disappointments, never accept defeat?

Looked at from the point of view of nature man is foolish. He does not fully trust the world he lives in. He has been waging war with it from the commencement of his history. He seems so fond of hurting himself from all directions. It is difficult to imagine how the careful mistress of natural selection should leave loopholes through which such unnecessary and dangerous elements could find entrance into her economy and encourage man to try to break the very world that sustains him. But the chick also behaves in the same unaccountably foolish manner in pecking through the wall of its little world. Somehow it has felt, with the accomplishment of an irresistible impulse, that there is something beyond its dear prison of shell waiting to give it the fulfilment of its existence in a manner it can never imagine.

In the same manner also, in his instinct, man is almost blindly sure that, however dense be his envelopment, he is to be born from Nature's womb to the world of spirit, — the world where he has his freedom of creation; where he is in coöperation with the infinite, where his creation and God's creation are to become one in harmony.

In almost all religious systems there is a large area of pessimism, where life has been held to be an evil, and the world a snare and a delusion; where man has felt himself to be furiously at war with his natural surroundings. He felt the oppression of all things so intensely that it seemed to him there was an evil personality in the world, which tempted him, and with all its cunning wiles waylaid him into destruction. In his desperation man had thought that he would shut up all possible communication with nature and utterly prove that he was sufficient in himself.

But this is the intensely painful antagonism of the child-life with the mother's life at the time of birth. It is cruel and destructive; it looks like ingratitude at the moment. And all religious pessimism is an ingratitude of deepest dye. It is a violent incitement to strike at that which has so long borne us and fed us with its own life.

Yet that there could be such an impossible paradox makes us pause and think. There are times when we detach ourselves from our history and believe that such pessimistic paroxysms were deliberate creations of certain monks and priests, who lived under unnatural conditions in a time of lawlessness. In such a belief we forget that conspiracies are creations of history, but history is no creation of conspiracies. There has been a violent demand upon human nature from its own depth to declare war against its own self. And though its violence has subsided, the battle-cry has not altogether ceased.

We must know that periods of transition have their language which cannot be taken literally. The first assertion of soul comes to man with too violent an emphasis upon the separateness from nature, against which it seems ready to carry out war of extermination. But it is the negative side. When the revolution for freedom breaks out, it takes the aspect of anarchy. Yet its true meaning is not in the destruction of government, but in the freedom of government.

In like manner, the soul's birth in the spiritual world is not the severance of relationship with what we call nature, but freedom of relationship, perfectness of realization.

In nature we are blind and lame like a child before its birth. But in the spiritual life we are born in freedom. And then because we are freed from the blind bondage of nature she is illuminated to us, and where we saw before mere envelopment we now see the mother.

But what is the ultimate end of the freedom which has come into man's life? It must have its meaning in something beyond which the question need go no farther. The answer is the same that we receive from the life of the animal if we ask what is its final meaning. The animals, by feeding and gratifying their desires, realize their own selves. And that is the ultimate end, to know that I am. The animal knows it, but its knowledge is like the smoke, not like the fire — it comes with a blind feeling but no illumination and though it arouses the truth it darkens it. It is the consciousness from the undistinguished non-self to the distinct self. It has just enough circumference to feel itself as the centre.

The ultimate end of freedom is also to know that "I am." But it is the liberation of man's consciousness from the separateness of the self into its unity with all. This freedom is not perfect in its mere extension, but its true perfection is in its intensity, which is love. The freedom of the child's birth from its mother's womb is not fulfilled by its fuller consciousness of its mother but in its intense consciousness of its mother in love. In the womb it was fed and was warm, but it was narrowly self-contained in its loneliness. After its birth, through the medium of its freedom, the inter-communication of the love of the mother and the child brings to the child the joy of the fullest consciousness of its personality. This mother's love gives to it the meaning of all its world. If the child were merely a feeding organism, then by fixing its roots into its world it could thrive. But the child is a person, and its personality needs its full realization, which can never be in the bondage of the womb. It has to be free, and the freedom of personality has its fulfilment, not in itself, but in other personality, and this is love.

It is not true that animals do not feel love. But it is too feeble to illuminate consciousness to such a degree as to reveal the whole truth of love to them. Their love has a glow which brightens their selves but has not the flame which goes beyond the mystery of personality. Its range is too immediately near to indicate its direction towards the paradox, that personality, which is the sense of unity in one's own self, yet which finds its real truth in its relationship of unity with others.

This paradox has led man to realize further that nature, into which we are born, is merely an imperfect truth, like the truth of the womb. But the full truth is, that we are born in the lap of the infinite personality. Our true world is not the world of the laws of matter and force, but the world of personality. When we fully realize it, our freedom is fulfilled. Then we understand what the Upanishat says, —

"Know all that moves in the moving world as enveloped by God, and enjoy by what he renounces."

We have seen that consciousness of personality begins with the feeling of the separateness from all and has its culmination in the feeling of the unity with all. It is needless to say that with the consciousness of separation there must be consciousness of unity, for it cannot exist solely by itself. But the life in which the consciousness of separation takes the first place and the unity the second place, and therefore where the personality is narrow and dim in the light of truth — this is the life of self. But the life in which the consciousness of unity is the primary and separateness the secondary factor, and therefore the personality is large and bright in truth, — this is the life of soul. The whole object of man is to free his personality of self into the personality of soul, to turn his inward forces into the forward movement towards the infinite, from the contraction of self in desire into the expansion of soul in love.

This personality, which is the conscious principle of oneness, the centre of relationships, is the reality, — therefore the ultimate object of attainment. I must emphasize this fact that this world is a real world only in its relation to a central personality. When that centre is taken away, then it falls to pieces, becomes a heap of abstractions, matter and force, logical symbols, and even those, — the thinnest semblances of reality, — would vanish into absolute nothingness, if the logical person in the centre, to whom they are related in some harmony of reason, were nowhere.

But these centres are innumerable. Each creature has its own little world related to its own personality. Therefore, the question naturally comes to our mind, — is the reality many, irreconcilably different each from the other.

If we have to give an answer in the affirmative, our whole nature rebels. For we know that in us the principle of oneness is the basis of all reality. Therefore, through all his questionings and imaginings from the dim dawn of his doubtings and debates, man has come to the truth, that there is one infinite centre to which all the personalities, and therefore all the world of reality, are related. He is "Mahāntam purusham," the one Supreme Person; he is "Satyam," the one Supreme Reality; he is "Jnanam," he has the knowledge in him of all knowers, therefore he knows himself in all knowings; he is "Sarvānubhuh," he feels in him the feelings of all creatures, therefore he feels himself in all feelings.

But this Supreme Person, the centre of all reality, is not merely a passive, a negatively receptive being. — Ananda-rupam amrtam yad vibhāti. He is the joy which reveals itself in forms. It is his will which creates.

Will has its supreme response, not in the world of law, but in the world of freedom, not in the world of nature, but in the spiritual world.

This we know in ourselves. Our slaves do our bidding, furnish us with our necessaries, but in them our relation is not perfect. We have our own freedom of will which can only find its true harmony in the freedom of other wills. Where we are slaves ourselves, in our selfish desires, we feel satisfaction in slaves. For slaves reflect our own slavery, which comes back to us, making us dependent. Therefore when America freed her slaves she truly freed herself, not only from the spiritual, but also from the material slavery. Our highest joy is in love. For there we realize the freedom of will in others. In friends, the will meets our will in fulness of freedom, not in coercion of want or fear; therefore, in this love, our personality finds its highest realization.

Because the truth of our will is in its freedom, therefore all our pure joy is in freedom. We have pleasure in the fulfilment of our necessity, — but this pleasure is of a negative nature. For necessity is a bondage, the fulfilment of which frees us from it. But there comes its end. It is different with our delight in beauty. It is of a positive nature. In the rhythm of harmony, whatever may be its reason, we find perfection. There we see not the substance, or the law, but some relationship of forms which has its harmony with our personality. From the bondage of mere lines and matter comes out that which is above all limitations — it is the complete unity of relationship. We at once feel free from the tyranny of unmeaningness of isolated things, — they now give us something which is personal to our own self. The revelation of unity in its passive perfection, which we find in nature, is beauty; the revelation of unity in its active perfection, which we find in the spiritual world, is love. This is not in the rhythm of proportions, but in the rhythm of wills. The will, which is free, must seek for the realization of its harmony other wills which are also free, and in this is the significance of spiritual life. The infinite centre of personality, which radiates its joy by giving itself out in freedom, must create other centres of freedom to unite with it in harmony. Beauty is the harmony realized in things which are bound by law. Love is the harmony realized in wills which are free.

In man, these centres of freedom have been created. It is not for him to be merely the recipient of favours from nature; he must fully radiate himself out in his creation of power and perfection of love. His movement must be towards the Supreme Person, whose movement is towards him. The creation of the natural world is God's own creation, we can only receive it and by receiving it make it our own. But in the creation of the spiritual world we are God's partners. In this work God has to wait for our will to harmonize with his own. It is not power which builds this spiritual world; there is no passivity in its remotest corner, no coercion. Consciousness has to be made clear of all mists of delusion, will has to be made free from all contrary forces of passions and desires, and then we meet with God where he creates. There can be no passive union, — because he is not a passive being. With him our relationship as that of a mere receiver of gifts is not fully true, for that is a onesided and therefore imperfect relationship. He gives us from his own fulness and we also give him from our abundance. And in this, not only is true joy for us, but for God also.

In our country the Vaishnavas have realized this truth and boldly asserted it by saying that God has to rely on human souls for the fulfilment of his love. In love there must be freedom, therefore God has not only to wait till our souls, out of their own will, bring themselves into harmony with his own, but also to suffer when there are obstacles and rebellions.

Therefore in the creation of the spiritual world, in which man has to work in union with God, there have been sufferings of which animals can have no idea. In the tuning of the instruments discords have shrieked loud, and strings have often snapped. When seen from this aspect, such work of collaboration between man and God has seemed as though meaninglessly malevolent. Because of the ideal that there is in the heart of this creation, every mistake and misfit has come as a stab and the world of soul has bled and groaned. Freedom has often taken the negative course to prove that it is freedom, — and man has suffered and God with him, so that this world of spirit might come out of its bath of fire, naked and pure, radiating light in all its limbs like a divine child. There have been hypocrisies and lies, cruel arrogance angered at the wounds it inflicts, spiritual pride that uses God's name to insult man, and pride of power that insults God by calling him its ally; there has been the smothered cry of centuries in pain robbed of its voice, and children of men mutilated of their right arms of strength to keep them helpless for all time; luxuries have been cultivated upon fields manured by the bloody sweat of slavery, and wealth built upon the foundations of penury and famines. But, I ask, has this giant spirit of negation won? Has it not its greatest defeat in the suffering it has caused in the heart of the infinite? and is not its callous pride shamed by the very grass of the wayside and flowers of the field every moment of its bloated existence? Does not the crime against man and God carry its own punishment upon its head in its crown of hideousness? Yes, the divine in man is not afraid of success, or of organization; it does not believe in the precautions of prudence and dimensions of power. Its strength is not in the muscle or the machine, neither in cleverness of policy nor in callousness of conscience; it is in its spirit of perfection. The to-day scoffs at it, but it has the eternity of to-morrow on its side. In appearance it is helpless like a babe, but its tears of suffering in the night set in motion all the unseen powers of heaven, the Mother in all creation is awakened. Prison walls break down, piles of wealth come tumbling to the dust under the weight of its huge disproportion. The history of the earth is the history of earthquakes and floods and volcanic fires, and yet, through it all, it is the history of the green fields and bubbling streams, of beauty and of prolific life. The spiritual world, which is being built of man's life and that of God, will pass its infancy of helpless falls and bruises, and one day will stand firm in its vigour of youth, glad in its own beauty and freedom of movement.

Our greatest hope is in this, that suffering is there. It is the language of imperfection. Its very utterance carries in it the trust in the perfect, like the baby's cry which would be dumb, if it had no faith in the mother. This suffering has driven man with his prayer knocking at the gate of the infinite in him, the divine, thus revealing his deepest instinct, his unreasoning faith in the reality of the ideal, — the faith shown in the readiness for death, in the renunciation of all that belongs to the self. God's life flowing in its outpour of self-giving has touched man's life who is also abroad in his career of freedom. When the discord rings out, man cries, — "asato ma sad gamaya." Help me to pass through the unreal to the real. It is the surrender of his self to be tuned for the music of the soul. This surrender is waited for, because the spiritual harmony cannot be effected except through freedom. Therefore man's willing surrender to the infinite is the commencement of the union. Only then can God's love fully act upon man's soul through the medium of freedom. This surrender is our soul's free choice of its life of coöperation with God, — coöperation in the work of the perfect moulding of the world of law into the world of love.

In the history of man moments have come when we have heard the music of God's life touching man's life in perfect harmony. We have known the fulfilment of man's personality in gaining God's nature for itself in utter self-giving out of abundance of love. Men have been born in this world of nature, with our human limitations and appetites, yet they proved that they breathed in the world of spirit, that the highest reality was the freedom of personality in the perfect union of love. They freed themselves pure from all selfish desires, from all narrowness of race and nationality, from the fear of man and the bondage of creeds and conventions. They became one with their God in the free active life of the infinite, in their unlimited abundance of renunciation. They suffered and loved. They received in their breasts the hurts of the evil of the world and proved that the life of the spirit was immortal. Great kingdoms change their shapes and vanish like clouds, institutions fade in the air like dreams, nations play their parts and disappear in obscurity, but these individuals carry the deathless life of all humanity in themselves. Their ceaseless life flows like a river of a mighty volume of flood, through the green fields and deserts, through the long dark caverns of oblivion into the dancing joy of the sunlight, bringing water of life to the door of multitudes of men through endless years, healing and allaying thirst and cleansing the impurities of the daily dust, and singing, with living voice, through the noise of the markets the song of the everlasting life, — the song which runs thus:

> "That is the Supreme Path of This.
> That is the Supreme Treasure of This.
> That is the Supreme World of This.
> That is the Supreme Joy of This."

MY SCHOOL

MY SCHOOL

I STARTED a school in Bengal when I was nearing forty. Certainly this was never expected of me, having spent the greater portion of my life in writing, chiefly verses. Therefore people naturally thought that as a school it might not be one of the best of its kind, but it was sure to be something outrageously new, being the product of daring inexperience.

This is one of the reasons why I am often asked what is the idea upon which my school is based. The question is a very embarrassing one for me because to satisfy the expectation of my questioners I cannot afford to be commonplace in my answer. However, I shall resist the temptation to be original and shall be content with being merely truthful.

In the first place I must confess it is difficult for me to say what is the idea underlying my institution. For the idea is not like a fixed foundation upon which a building is erected. It is more like a seed which cannot be separated and pointed out directly it begins to grow into a plant.

And I know what it was to which this school owes its origin. It was not any new theory of education, but the memory of my school days.

That those days were unhappy ones for me I cannot altogether ascribe to my peculiar temperament or to any special demerit of the schools to which I was sent. It may be that if I had been a little less sensitive, I could gradually have accommodated myself to its pressure and survived long enough to earn my university degrees. But all the same, schools are schools, though some are better and some worse, according to their own standard.

The provision has been made for the infants to be fed upon their mother's milk. They find their food and their mother at the same time. It is complete nourishment for them, body and soul. It is their first introduction to the great truth that man's true relationship with the world is that of personal love and not that of the mechanical law of causation.

The introduction and the conclusion of a book have a similarity of features. In both places the complete aspect of truth is given. Only in the introduction it is simple because undeveloped, and in the conclusion it becomes simple again because perfectly developed. Truth has the middle course of its career, where it grows complex, where it hurts itself against obstacles, breaks itself into pieces to find itself back in a fuller unity of realization.

Similarly man's introduction to this world is his introduction to his final truth in a simple form. He is born into a world which to him is intensely living, where he as an individual occupies the full attention of his surroundings. Then he grows up to doubt this deeply personal aspect of reality, he loses himself in the complexity of things, separates himself from his surroundings, often in a spirit of antagonism. But this shattering of the unity of truth, this uncompromising civil war between his personality and his outer world, can never find its meaning in interminable discord. Thereupon to find the true conclusion of his life he has to come back through this digression of doubt to the simplicity of perfect truth, to his union with all in an infinite bond of love.

Therefore our childhood should be given its full measure of life's draught, for which it has an endless thirst. The young mind should be saturated with the idea that it has been born in a human world which is in harmony with the world around it. And this is what our regular type of school ignores with an air of superior wisdom, severe and disdainful. It forcibly snatches away children from a world full of the mystery of God's own handiwork, full of the suggestiveness of personality. It is a mere method of discipline which refuses to take into account the individual. It is a manufactory specially designed for grinding out uniform results. It follows an imaginary straight line of the average in digging its channel of education. But life's line is not the straight line, for it is fond of playing the seesaw with the line of the average, bringing upon its head the rebuke of the school. For according to the school life is perfect when it allows itself to be treated as dead, to be cut into symmetrical conveniences. And this was the cause of my suffering when I was sent to school. For all of a sudden I found my world vanishing from around me, giving place to wooden benches and straight walls staring at me with the blank stare of the blind. I was not a creation of the schoolmaster, — the Government Board of Education was not consulted when I took birth in the world. But was that any reason why they should wreak their vengeance upon me for this oversight of my creator?

But the legend is that eating of the fruit of knowledge is not consonant with dwelling in paradise. Therefore men's children have to be banished from their paradise into a realm of death, dominated by the decency of a tailoring department. So my mind had to accept the tight-fitting encasement of the school which, being like the shoes of a mandarin woman, pinched and bruised my nature on all sides and at every movement. I was fortunate enough in extricating myself before insensibility set in.

Though I did not have to serve the full penal term which men of my position have to undergo to find their entrance into cultured society, I am glad that I did not altogether escape from its molestation. For it has given me knowledge of the wrong from which the children of men suffer.

The cause of it is this, that man's intention is going against God's intention as to how children should grow into knowledge. How we should conduct our business is our own affair, and therefore in our offices we are free to create in the measure of our special purposes. But such office arrangement does not suit God's creation. And children are God's own creation.

We have come to this world to accept it, not merely to know it. We may become powerful by knowledge, but we attain fulness by sympathy. The highest education is that which does not merely give us information but makes our life in harmony with all existence. But we find that this education of sympathy is not only systematically ignored in schools, but it is severely repressed. From our very childhood habits are formed and knowledge is imparted in such a manner that our life is weaned away from nature and our mind and the world are set in opposition from the beginning of our days. Thus the greatest of educations for which we came prepared is neglected, and we are made to lose our world to find a bagful of informations instead. We rob the child of his earth to teach him geography, of language to teach him grammar. His hunger is for the Epic, but he is supplied with chronicles of facts and dates. He was born in the human world, but is banished into the world of living gramophones, to expiate for the original sin of being born in ignorance. Child-nature protests against such calamity with all its power of suffering, subdued at last into silence by punishment.

We all know children are lovers of the dust; their whole body and mind thirst for sunlight and air as flowers do. They are never in a mood to refuse the constant invitations to establish direct communication coming to their senses from the universe.

But unfortunately for children their parents,

in the pursuit of their profession, in conformity to their social traditions, live in their own peculiar world of habits. Much of this cannot be helped. For men have to specialize, driven by circumstances and by need of social uniformity.

But our childhood is the period when we have or ought to have more freedom — freedom from the necessity of specialization into the narrow bounds of social and professional conventionalism.

I well remember the surprise and annoyance of an experienced headmaster, reputed to be a successful disciplinarian, when he saw one of the boys of my school climbing a tree and choosing a fork of the branches for settling down to his studies. I had to say to him in explanation that "childhood is the only period of life when a civilized man can exercise his choice between the branches of a tree and his drawing-room chair, and should I deprive this boy of that privilege because I, as a grown-up man, am barred from it?" What is surprising is to notice the same headmaster's approbation of the boys' studying Botany. He believes in an impersonal knowledge

AT COLORADO SPRINGS, COLORADO

of the tree because that is science, but not in a personal experience of it. This growth of experience leads to forming instinct which is the result of nature's own method of instruction. The boys of my school have acquired instinctive knowledge of the physiognomy of the tree. By the least touch they know where they can find a foothold upon an apparently inhospitable trunk; they know how far they can take liberty with the branches, how to distribute their bodies' weight so as to make themselves least burdensome to branchlets. My boys are able to make the best possible use of the tree in the matter of gathering fruits, taking rest and hiding from undesirable pursuers. I myself was brought up in a cultured home in a town, and as far as my personal behaviour goes I have been obliged to act all through my life as if I were born in a world where there are no trees. Therefore I consider it as a part of education for my boys to let them fully realize that they are in a scheme of existence where trees are a substantial fact, not merely as generating chlorophyl and taking carbon from the air, but as living trees.

Naturally the soles of our feet are so made that they become the best instruments for us to stand upon the earth and to walk with. From the day we commenced to wear shoes we minimized the purpose of our feet. With the lessening of their responsibility they have lost their dignity, and now they lend themselves to be pampered with socks, slippers and shoes of all prices and shapes and misproportions. For us it amounts to a grievance against God for not giving us hooves instead of beautifully sensitive soles.

I am not for banishing foot-gear altogether from men's use. But I have no hesitation in asserting that the soles of children's feet should not be deprived of their education, provided for them by nature, free of cost. Of all the limbs we have they are the best adapted for intimately knowing the earth by their touch. For the earth has her subtle modulations of contour which she only offers for the kiss of her true lovers — the feet.

I have again to confess that I was brought up in a respectable household and my feet from childhood have carefully been saved from all naked contact with the dust. When I try to emulate my boys in walking barefoot, I painfully realize what thickness of ignorance about the earth I carry under my feet. I invariably choose the thorns to tread upon in such a manner as to make the thorns exult. My feet do not have the instinct to follow the lines of least resistance. For even the flattest of earth-surfaces has its dimples of diminutive hills and dales only discernible by educated feet. I have often wondered at the unreasonable zigzag of footpaths across perfectly plain fields. It becomes all the more perplexing when you consider that a footpath is not made by the caprice of one individual. Unless most of the walkers possessed exactly the same eccentricity such obviously inconvenient passages could not have been made. But the real cause lies in the subtle suggestions coming from the earth to which our feet unconsciously respond. Those for whom such communications have not been cut off can adjust their muscles of the feet with great rapidity at the least indication. Therefore they can save themselves from the intrusion of thorns, even while treading upon them, and walk barefooted on a gravelly path without the least discomfort. I know that in the practical world shoes will be worn, roads will be metalled, cars will be used. But during their period of education should children be not given to know that the world is not all drawing-room, that there is such a thing as nature to which their limbs are made beautifully to respond?

There are men who think that by the simplicity of living, introduced in my school, I preach the idealization of poverty which prevailed in the mediæval age. The full discussion of this subject is outside the scope of my paper, but seen from the point of view of education, should we not admit that poverty is the school in which man had his first lessons and his best training? Even a millionnaire's son has to be born helplessly poor and to begin his lesson of life from the beginning. He has to learn to walk like the poorest of children, though he has means to afford to be without the appendage of legs. Poverty brings us into complete touch with life and the world, for living richly is living mostly by proxy, thus living in a lesser world of reality. This may be good for one's pleasure and pride, but not for one's education. Wealth is a golden cage in which the children of the rich are bred into artificial deadening of their powers. Therefore in my school, much to the disgust of the people of expensive habits, I had to provide for this great teacher, — this bareness of furniture and materials, — not because it is poverty, but because it leads to personal experience of the world.

What I propose is that men should have some limited period of their life specially reserved for the life of the primitive man. Civilized busybodies have not been allowed to tamper with the unborn child. In the mother's womb it has leisure to finish its first stage of the vegetative life. But directly it is born with all its instincts ready for the next stage, which is the natural life, it is at once pounced upon by the society of cultivated habits to be snatched away from the open arms of the earth, water and the sky, from the sunlight and air. At first it struggles and bitterly cries, and then it gradually forgets that it had for its inheritance God's creation; then it shuts its windows, pulls down its curtains, loses itself among meaningless miscellanies and feels proud of its accumulations at the cost of its world and possibly of its soul.

The civilized world of conventions and things comes in the middle career of man's progress. It is neither in the beginning nor in the end. Its enormous complexity and codes of decorum have their uses. But when it takes these to be final, and makes it a rule that no green spot should be left in man's life away from its reign of smoke and noise, of draped and decorated propriety, then children suffer, and in the young men is produced world-weariness, and old men forget to grow old in peace and beauty, merely becoming dilapidated youths, ashamed of their shabbiness of age, full of holes and patchwork.

However, it is certain that children did not bargain for this muffled and screened world of decency when they were ready to be born upon this earth. If they had any idea that they were about to open their eyes to the sunlight, only to find themselves in the hands of the education department till they should lose their freshness of mind and keenness of sense, they would think twice before venturing upon their career of humanity. God's arrangements are never insolently special arrangements. They always have the harmony of wholeness and unbroken continuity with all things. Therefore what tortured me in my school days was the fact that the school had not the completeness of the world. It was a special arrangement for giving lessons. It could only be suitable for grown-up people who were conscious of the special need of such places and therefore ready to accept their teaching at the cost of dissociation from life. But children are in love with life, and it is their first love. All its colour and movement attracts their eager attention. And are we quite sure of our wisdom in stifling this love? Children are not born ascetics, fit to enter at once into the monastic discipline of acquiring knowledge. At first they must gather knowledge through their love of life, and then they will renounce their lives to gain knowledge, and then again they will come back to their fuller lives with ripened wisdom.

But society has made its own arrangements for manipulating men's minds to fit its special patterns. These arrangements are so closely organized that it is difficult to find gaps through which to bring in nature. There is a serial adjustment of penalties which follows to the end one who ventures to take liberty with some part of the arrangements, even to save his soul. Therefore it is one thing to realize truth and another to bring it into practice where the whole current of the prevailing system goes against you. This is why when I had to face the problem of my own son's education I was at a loss to give it a practical solution. The first thing that I did was to take him away from the town surroundings into a village and allow him the freedom of primeval nature as far as it is available in modern days. He had a river, noted for its danger, where he swam and rowed without check from the anxiety of his elders. He spent his time in the fields and on the trackless sand banks, coming late for his meals without being questioned. He had none of those luxuries that are not only customary but are held as proper for boys of his circumstance. For which privations, I am sure, he was pitied and his parents blamed by the people for whom society has blotted out the whole world. But I was certain that luxuries are burdens to boys. They are the burdens of other people's habits, the burdens of the vicarious pride and pleasure which parents enjoy through their children.

Yet, being an individual of limited resources, I could do very little for my son in the way of educating him according to my plan. But he had freedom of movement, he had very few of the screens of wealth and respectability between himself and the world of nature. Thus he had a better opportunity for a real experience of this universe than I ever had. But one thing exercised my mind more than anything else as the most important.

The object of education is to give man the unity of truth. Formerly, when life was simple, all the different elements of man were in complete harmony. But when there came the separation of the intellect from the spiritual and the physical, the school education put entire emphasis on the intellect and on the physical side of man. We devote our sole attention to giving children information, not knowing that by this emphasis we are accentuating a break between the intellectual, the physical and the spiritual life.

I believe in a spiritual world — not as anything separate from this world — but as its innermost truth. With the breath we draw we must always feel this truth, that we are living in God. Born in this great world, full of the mystery of the infinite, we cannot accept our existence as a momentary outburst of chance drifting on the current of matter towards an eternal nowhere. We cannot look upon our lives as dreams of a dreamer who has no awakening in all time. We have a personality to which matter and force are unmeaning unless related to something infinitely personal, whose nature we have discovered, in some measure, in human love, in the greatness of the good, in the martyrdom of heroic souls, in the ineffable beauty of nature which can never be a mere physical fact nor anything but an expression of personality.

Experience of this spiritual world, whose reality we miss by our incessant habit of ignoring it from childhood, has to be gained by children by fully living in it and not through the medium of theological instruction. But how this is to be done is a problem difficult of solution in the present age. For nowadays men have managed so fully to occupy their time that they do not find leisure to know that their activities have only movement but very little truth, that their soul has not found its world.

In India we still cherish in our memory the tradition of the forest colonies of great teachers. These places were neither schools nor monasteries, in the modern sense of the word. They consisted of homes where with their families lived men whose object was to see the world in God and to realize their own life in him. Though they lived outside society, yet they were to society what the sun is to the planets, the centre from which it received its life and light. And here boys grew up in an intimate vision of eternal life before they were thought fit to enter the state of the householder.

Thus in the ancient India the school was there where was the life itself. There the students were brought up, not in the academic atmosphere of scholarship and learning, or in the maimed life of monastic seclusion, but in the atmosphere of living aspiration. They took the cattle to pasture, collected firewood, gathered fruit, cultivated kindness to all creatures and grew in their spirit with their own teachers' spiritual growth. This was possible because the primary object of these places was not teaching but giving shelter to those who lived their life in God.

That this traditional relationship of the masters and disciples is not a mere romantic fiction is proved by the relic we still possess of the indigenous system of education which has preserved its independence for centuries to be about to succumb at last to the hand of the foreign bureaucratic control. These *chatus-pathis*, which is the Sanskrit name for the university, have not the savour of the school about them. The students live in their master's home like the children of the house, without having to pay for their board and lodging or tuition. The teacher prosecutes his own study, living a life of simplicity, and helping the students in their lessons as a part of his life and not of his profession.

This ideal of education through sharing a life of high aspiration with one's master took possession of my mind. The narrowness of our caged up future and the sordidness of our maimed opportunities urged me all the more towards its realization. Those who in other countries are favoured with unlimited expectations of worldly prospects can fix their purposes of education to those objects. The range of their life is varied and wide enough to give them the freedom necessary for development of their powers. But for us to maintain our self-respect which we owe to ourselves and to our creator, we must make the purpose of our education nothing short of the highest purpose of man, the fullest growth and freedom of soul. It is pitiful to have to scramble for small pittances of fortune. Only let us have access to the life that goes beyond death and rises above all circumstances, let us find our God, let us live for that ultimate truth which emancipates us from the bondage of the dust and gives us the wealth, not of things but of inner light, not of power but of love. Such emancipation of soul we have witnessed in our country among men devoid of book-learning and living in absolute poverty. In India we have the inheritance of this treasure of spiritual wisdom. Let the object of our education be to open it out before us and to give us the power to make the true use of it in our life, and offer it to the rest of the world when the time comes, as our contribution to its eternal welfare.

I had been immersed in literary activities when this thought struck my mind with painful intensity. I suddenly felt like one groaning under the suffocation of nightmare. It was not only my own soul, but the soul of my country that seemed to be struggling for its breath through me. I felt clearly that what was needed was not any particular material object, not wealth or comfort or power, but our awakening to full consciousness in soul freedom, the freedom of the life in God, where we have no enmity with those who must fight, no competition with those who must make money, where we are beyond all attacks and above all insults.

Fortunately for me I had a place ready to my hand where I could begin my work. My father, in one of his numerous travels, had selected this lonely spot as the one suitable for his life of communion with God. This place, with a permanent endowment, he dedicated to the use of those who seek peace and seclusion for their meditation and prayer. I had about ten boys with me when I came here and started my new life with no previous experience whatever.

All round our ashram is a vast open country, bare up to the line of the horizon except for sparsely growing stunted date palms and prickly shrubs struggling with ant-hills. Below the level of the field there extend numberless mounds and tiny hillocks of red gravel and pebbles of all shapes and colours, intersected by narrow channels of rainwater. Not far away towards the south near the village can be seen through the intervals of a row of palm trees the gleaming surface of steel-blue water, collected in a hollow of the ground. A road used by the village people for their marketing in the town goes meandering through the lonely fields, with its red dust staring in the sun. Travellers coming up this road can see from a distance on the summit of the undulating ground the spire of a temple and the top of a building, indicating the Shanti-Niketan ashram, among its *amalaki* groves and its avenue of stately sal trees.

And here the school has been growing up for over fifteen years, passing through many changes and often grave crises. Having the evil reputation of a poet, I could with great difficulty win the trust of my countrymen and avoid the suspicion of the bureaucracy. That at last I have been able to accomplish it in some measure is owing to my never expecting it, going on in my own way without waiting for outside sympathy, help or advice. My resources were extremely small, with the burden of a heavy debt upon them. But this poverty itself gave me the full strength of freedom, making me rely upon truth rather than upon materials.

Because the growth of this school was the growth of my life and not that of a mere carrying out of my doctrines, its ideals changed with its maturity like a ripening fruit that not only grows in its bulk and deepens in its colour, but undergoes change in the very quality of its inner pulp. I started with the idea that I had a benevolent object to perform. I worked hard, but the only satisfaction I had came from keeping count of the amount of sacrifice in money, energy and time; admiring my own untiring goodness. But the result achieved was of small worth. I went on building system after system and then pulling them down. It merely occupied my time, but at the heart my work remained vacant. I well remember when an old disciple of my father came and said to me, "What I see about me, is like a wedding hall where nothing is wanting in preparation, only the bridegroom is absent." The mistake I made was in thinking that my own purpose was that bridegroom. But gradually my heart found its centre. It was not in the work, not in my wish, but in truth. I sat alone on the upper terrace of the Shanti-Niketan house and gazed upon the tree tops of the *sal* avenue before me. I withdrew my heart from my own schemes and calculations, from my daily struggles, and held it up in silence before the peace and presence that permeated the sky; and gradually my heart was filled. I began to see the world around me through the sight of my soul. The trees seemed to me like silent hymns rising from the mute heart of the earth, and the shouts and laughter of the boys mingling in the evening sky came before me like trees of living sounds rising up from the depth of human life. I found my message in the sunlight that touched my inner mind and felt a fullness in the sky that spoke to me in the word of our ancient rishi, — "Ko hyevānyāt, Kah prānyāt yadesha ākāsha ānando no syāt"—"Whoever could move and strive and live in this world if the sky were not filled with love?" Thus when I turned back from the struggle to achieve results, from the ambition of doing benefit to others, and came to my own innermost need, when I felt that living one's own life in truth is living the life of all the world, then the unquiet atmosphere of the outward struggle cleared up and the power of spontaneous creation found its way through the centre of all things. Even now whatever is superficial and futile in the working of our institution is owing to distrust of the spirit, lurking in our mind, to the ineradicable consciousness of our self-importance, to the habit of looking for the cause of our failures outside us, and the endeavour to repair all looseness in our work by tightening the screws of organization. From my experience I know that where the eagerness to teach others is too strong, especially in the matter of spiritual life, the result becomes meagre and mixed with untruth. All the hypocrisy and self-delusion in our religious convictions and practices are the outcome of the goadings of overzealous activities of mentorship. In our spiritual attainment gaining and giving are the same thing; as in a lamp, to light itself is the same as to impart light to others. When a man makes it his profession to preach God to others, then he will raise the dust more than give direction to truth. Teaching of religion can never be imparted in the form of lessons, it is there where there is religion in living. Therefore the ideal of the forest colony of the seekers of God as the true school of spiritual life holds good even in this age. Religion is not a fractional thing that can be doled out in fixed weekly or daily measures as one among various subjects in the school syllabus. It is the truth of our complete being, the consciousness of our personal relationship with the infinite; it is the true centre of gravity of our life. This we can attain during our childhood by daily living in a place where the truth of the spiritual world is not obscured by a crowd of necessities assuming artificial importance; where life is simple, surrounded by fulness of leisure, by ample space and pure air and profound peace of nature; and where men live with a perfect faith in the eternal life before them.

But the question will be asked whether I have attained my ideal in this institution. My answer is that the attainment of all our deepest ideals is difficult to measure by outward standards. Its working is not immediately perceptible by results. We have fully admitted the inequalities and varieties of human life in our *ashram*. We never try to gain some kind of outward uniformity by weeding out the differences of nature and training of our members. Some of us belong to the Brahma Samaj sect and some to other sects of Hinduism; and some of us are Christians. Because we do not deal with creeds and dogmas of sectarianism, therefore this heterogeneity of our religious beliefs does not present us with any difficulty whatever. This also I know, that the feeling of respect for the ideal of this place and the life lived here greatly varies in depth and earnestness among those who have gathered in this *ashram*. I know that our aspiration for a higher life has not risen far above our greed for worldly goods and reputation. Yet I am perfectly certain, and proofs of it are numerous, that the ideal of the *ashram* is sinking deeper and deeper into our nature every day. The tuning of our life's strings into purer spiritual notes is going on without our being aware of it. Whatever might be our original motive in coming here, the call sounds without ceasing through all our clamour of discords, the call of *shāntam*, *shivam*, *advaitam*, — the All Peace, the All Good, and the One. The sky here seems penetrated with the voice of the infinite, making the peace of its daybreak and stillness of its night profound with meaning, and sending through the white crowds of *shiuli* flowers in the autumn and *malati* in the summer, the message of self-dedication in the perfect beauty of worship.

It will be difficult for others than Indians to realize all the associations that are grouped round the word *ashram*, the forest sanctuary. For it blossomed in India like its own lotus, under a sky generous in its sunlight and starry splendour. India's climate has brought to us the invitation of the open air; the language of her mighty rivers is solemn in their chants; the limitless expanse of her plains encircles our homes with the silence of the world beyond; there the sun rises from the marge of the green earth like an offering of the unseen to the altar of the Unknown, and it goes down to the west at the end of the day like a gorgeous ceremony of nature's salutation to the Eternal. In India the shades of the trees are hospitable, the dust of the earth stretches its brown arms to us, the air with its embraces clothes us with warmth. These are the unchanging facts that ever carry their suggestions to our minds, and therefore we feel it is India's mission to realize the truth of the human soul in the Supreme Soul through its union with the soul of the world. This mission had taken its natural form in the forest schools in the ancient time. And it still urges us to seek for the vision of the infinite in all forms of creation, in the human relationships of love, to feel it in the air we breathe, in the light in which we open our eyes, in the water in which we bathe, in the earth on which we live and die. Therefore I know — and I know it from my own experience, — that the students and the teachers who have come together in this *ashram* are daily growing towards the emancipation of their minds into the consciousness of the infinite, not through any process of teaching or outer discipline, but by the help of an unseen atmosphere of aspiration that surrounds the place and the memory of a devoted soul who lived here in intimate communion with God.

I hope I have been able to explain how the conscious purpose that led me to found my school in the *ashram* gradually lost its independence and grew into unity with the purpose that reigns in this place. In a word my work found its soul in the spirit of the *ashram*. But that soul has its outer form, no doubt, which is its aspect of the school. And in the teaching system of this school I have been trying all these years to carry out my theory of education based upon my experience of children's minds.

I believe, as I suggested before, that children have their subconscious mind more active than their conscious intelligence. A vast quantity of the most important of our lessons has been taught to us through this. Experiences of countless generations have been instilled into our nature by its agency, not only without causing us any fatigue, but giving us joy. This subconscious faculty of knowledge is completely one with our life. It is not like a lantern that can be lighted and trimmed from outside, but it is like the light that the glow-worm possesses by the exercise of its life process.

Fortunately for me I was brought up in a family where literature, music and art had become instinctive. My brothers and cousins lived in the freedom of ideas, and most of them had natural artistic powers. Nourished in these surroundings, I began to think early and to dream and to put my thoughts into expression. In religion and social ideals our family was free from all convention, being ostracized by society owing to our secession from orthodox beliefs and customs. This made us fearless in our freedom of mind, and we tried experiments in all departments of life. This was the education I had in my early days, freedom and joy in the exercise of my mental and artistic faculties. And because this made my mind fully alive to grow in its natural environment of nutrition, therefore the grinding of school system became so extremely intolerable to me.

I had only this experience of my early life to help me when I started my school. I felt sure that what was most necessary was the breath of culture and no formal method of teaching. Fortunately for me, Satish Chandra Roy, a young student of great promise, who was getting ready for his B.A. degree, became attracted to my school and devoted his life to carry out my idea. He was barely nineteen, but he had a wonderful soul, living in a world of ideas, keenly responsive to all that was beautiful and great in the realm of nature and of human mind. He was a poet who would surely have taken his place among the immortals of world-literature if he had been spared to live, but he died when he was twenty, thus offering his service to our school only for the period of one short year. With him boys never felt that they were confined in the limit of a teaching class; they seemed to have their access to everywhere. They would go with him to the forest when in the spring the *sal* trees were in full blossom and he would recite to them his favorite poems, frenzied with excitement. He used to read to them Shakespeare and even Browning, — for he was a great lover of Browning, — explaining to them in Bengali with his wonderful power of expression. He never had any feeling of distrust for boys' capacity of understanding; he would talk and read to them about whatever was the subject in which he himself was interested. He knew that it was not at all necessary for the boys to understand literally and accurately, but that their minds should be roused, and in this he was always successful. He was not like other teachers, a mere vehicle of text-books. He made his teaching personal, he himself was the source of it, and therefore it was made of life stuff, easily assimilable by the living human nature. The real reason of his success was his intense interest in life, in ideas, in everything around him, in the boys who came in contact with him. He had his inspiration not through the medium of books, but through the direct communication of his sensitive mind with the world. The seasons had upon him the same effect as they had upon the plants. He seemed to feel in his blood the unseen messages of nature that are always travelling through space, floating in the air, shimmering in the sky, tingling in the roots of the grass under the earth. The literature that he studied had not the least smell of the library about it. He had the power to see ideas before him, as he could see his friends, with all the distinctness of form and subtlety of life.

Thus the boys of our school were fortunate enough to be able to receive their lessons from a living teacher and not from text-books. Have not our books, like most of our necessaries, come between us and our world? We have got into the habit of covering the windows of our minds with their pages, and plasters of book phrases have stuck into our mental skin, making it impervious of all direct touches of truth. A whole world of bookish truths have formed themselves into a strong citadel with rings of walls in which we have taken shelter, secured from the communication of God's creation. Of course, it would be foolish to underrate the advantages of the book. But at the same time we must admit that the book has its limitations and its dangers. At any rate during the early period of education children should come to their lesson of truths through natural processes — directly through persons and things.

Being convinced of this, I have set all my resources to create an atmosphere of ideas in the *ashram*. Songs are composed, not specially made to order for juvenile minds. They are songs that a poet writes for his own pleasure. In fact, most of my "Gitanjali" songs were written here. These, when fresh in their first bloom, are sung to the boys, and they come in crowds to learn them. They sing them in their leisure hours, sitting in groups, under the open sky on moonlight nights, in the shadows of the impending rain in July. All my latter-day plays have been written here, and the boys have taken part in their performance. Lyrical dramas have been written for their season-festivals. They have ready access to the room where I read to the teachers any new things that I write in prose or in verse, whatever the subject may be. And this they utilize without the least pressure put upon them, feeling aggrieved when not invited. A few weeks before leaving India I read to them Browning's drama "Luria," translating it into Bengali as I went on. It took me two evenings, but the second meeting was as full as the first one. Those who have witnessed these boys playing their parts in dramatic performances have been struck with their wonderful power as actors. It is because they are never directly trained in the histrionic art. They instinctively enter into the spirit of the plays in which they take part, though these plays are no mere school-boy dramas. They require subtle understanding and sympathy. With all the anxiety and hypercritical sensitiveness of an author about the performance of his own play I have never been disappointed in my boys, and I have rarely allowed teachers to interfere with the boys' own representation of the characters. Very often they themselves write plays or improvise them and we are invited to their performance. They hold meetings of their literary clubs and they have at least three illustrated magazines conducted by three sections of the school, the most interesting of them being that of the infant section. A number of our boys have shown remarkable powers in drawing and painting, developed not through the orthodox method of copying models, but by following their own bent and by the help of occasional visits from some artists to inspire the boys with their own work.

When I first started my school, my boys had no evident love for music. The consequence is that at the beginning I did not employ a music teacher and did not force the boys to take music lessons. I merely created opportunities when those of us who had the gift could exercise their musical culture. It had the effect of unconsciously training the ears of the boys. And when gradually most of them showed a strong inclination and love for music I saw that they would be willing to subject themselves to formal teaching, and it was then that I secured a music teacher.

In our school the boys rise very early in the morning, sometimes before it is light. They attend to the drawing of water for their bath. They make up their beds. They do all those things that tend to cultivate the spirit of self-help.

I believe in the hour of meditation, and I set aside fifteen minutes in the morning and fifteen minutes in the evening for that purpose. I insist on this period of meditation, not however expecting the boys to be hypocrites and to make believe they are meditating. But I do insist that they remain quiet, that they exert the power of self-control, even though instead of contemplating on God, they may be watching the squirrels running up the trees.

Any description of such a school is necessarily inadequate. For the most important element of it is the atmosphere, also the fact that it is not a school which is imposed upon the boys by autocratic authorities. I always try to impress upon their minds that it is their own world, upon which their life ought fully and freely to react. In the school administration they have their place, and in the matter of punishment we mostly rely upon their own court of justice.

In conclusion I warn my hearers not to carry away with them any false or exaggerated picture of this *ashram*. When ideas are stated in a paper, they appear too simple and complete. But in reality their manifestation through the materials that are living and varied and ever changing is not so clear and perfect. We have obstacles in human nature and in outer circumstances. Some of us have a feeble faith in boys' minds as living organisms, and some have the natural propensity of doing good by force. On the other hand, the boys have their different degrees of receptivity and there are a good number of inevitable failures. Delinquencies make their appearance unexpectedly, making us suspicious as to the efficacy of our own ideals. We pass through dark periods of doubt and reaction. But these conflicts and waverings belong to the true aspects of reality. Living ideals can never be set into a clockwork arrangement, giving accurate account of its every second. And those who have firm faith in their idea have to test its truth in discords and failures that are sure to come to tempt them from their path. I for my part believe in the principle of life, in the soul of man, more than in methods. I believe that the object of education is the freedom of mind which can only be achieved through the path of freedom — though freedom has its risk and responsibility as life itself has. I know it for certain, though most people seem to have forgotten it, that children are living beings — more living than grown-up people, who have built their shells of habit around them. Therefore it is absolutely necessary for their mental health and development that they must not have mere schools for their lessons, but a world whose guiding spirit is personal love. It must be an *ashram* where men have gathered for the highest end of life, in the peace of nature; where life is not merely meditative, but fully awake in its activities, where boys' minds are not being perpetually drilled into believing that the ideal of the self-idolatry of the nation is the truest ideal for them to accept; where they are bidden to realize man's world as God's Kingdom to whose citizenship they have to aspire; where the sunrise and sunset and the silent glory of stars are not daily ignored; where nature's festivities of flowers and fruit have their joyous recognition from man; and where the young and the old, the teacher and the student, sit at the same table to partake of their daily food and the food of their eternal life.

MEDITATION

MEDITATION

THERE are things that we get from outside and take to ourselves as possessions. But with meditation, it is just the opposite. It is entering into the very midst of some great truth, so that, in the end, we are possessed by it.

Now let us see by contrast what wealth is. Money represents so much labour. By its means I can detach the labour from man and make it my own possession. I acquire it from outside and convert it to my own power.

Then there is knowledge. One kind of knowledge is that which we gain from other men. Then there is the other kind which we acquire through observation, experiments and the process of reasoning.

These are all efforts to take that which is away from me, and get it to myself. In these things our mental and physical energies are employed in quite a contrary manner from in Meditation.

The highest truth is that which we can only realize by plunging into it. And when our consciousness is fully merged in it, then we know that it is no mere acquisition, but that we are one with it.

Thus through meditation, when our soul is in its true relation to the Supreme Truth, then all our actions, words, behaviour, become true.

Let me give you a text of meditation which we have used in India.

Om bhur bhuvah svah
    tat savitur varenyam bhargo devasya dhimahi
        dhiyo yo nah prachodayat.

OM. That means completeness; it is really the symbolical word meaning the Infinite, the Perfect, the Eternal. The very sound is complete, representing the wholeness of all things.

All our meditations begin with OM and end with OM. It is used so that the mind may be filled with the sense of the infinite Completeness and emancipated from the world of narrow selfishness.

Bhur bhuvah svah.

Bhuh means this earth.

Bhuvah means the middle region, the sky.

Svah means the starry region.

The earth, the air, the starry region. You have to set your mind in the heart of this universe. You have to realize that you are born in the Infinite, that you belong not merely to a particular spot of this earth, but to the whole world.

Tat savitur varenyam bhargo devasya dhimahi.

I meditate upon that adorable Energy of the Creator of the Universe. The word "Creator" has dulled in meaning by its constant use. But you have to bring into your conscious vision the vastness of the all, and then say that God creates this world, from his infinite creative power, at every moment of time continuously, not by a single act.

All this represents the infinite will of the Creator. It is not like the law of Gravitation, or some abstract thing which I cannot worship, and which cannot claim our worship. But this text says that the power is "adorable," that it claims our worship because it belongs to a supreme person, it is not a mere abstraction.

What is the manifestation of this power?

On one side it is the Earth, the Sky, the Starry Heavens; on the other side it is our consciousness.

There is an eternal connection between myself and the world, because this world has its other side in my consciousness. If there were no conscious being and no Supreme Consciousness at its source and centre, there could not be a world.

God's power emanates and streams forth as consciousness in me and also in the world outside. We ourselves generally divide it, but really these two sides of creation are intimately related as they proceed from the same source.

Thus this Meditation means that my consciousness and the vast world outside me are one. And where is that Unity?

In that Great Power, who breathes out Consciousness in me, and also in the world outside myself.

Meditation upon this is not taking anything

to myself, but renouncing myself, becoming one with all creation.

This then is our text and we set our minds to it, — repeating it again and again till our mind becomes settled and distractions leave us. There is then no loss, no fear, no pain that can affect us — our relationship with men becomes simple, natural — we are free. This then is the Meditation — to plunge into this truth, to live and move and have our being in this.

Let me tell you about another text which we use in our school for the boys to meditate upon and to use for their daily prayer.

Om pita no'si, pita no bodhi. Namaste'stu.

Pita no'si.

Thou art our Father.

Pita no bodhi. Give us the "bodh," the consciousness, the awakening in *this*, — that thou art our Father.

Namaste'stu.

Namah has no proper synonym in English, though perhaps "bow" or "salutation" gives its meaning as nearly as may be.

My namah to thee — Let it become true.

This is the first portion of the text, which our boys use.

Let me explain what I understand by it.

Pita no'si. The text begins with the assertion that God *is* our Father.

But this truth has not yet been realized in our life, and this is the cause of our imperfections, miseries and sins. Therefore we pray that we may be able to realize it in our consciousness, and so we pray that we may be able to do so.

Then it ends with "Namaste." Let my "Namah" be true. Because that Namah is the *true* attitude. When I have fully realized this great truth, — Pita no'si, — then my life expresses its own truth by its Namah, by its humility, by its self-surrender, in the meek feeling of adoration.

In our prayers we sometimes use words which satisfy us though we merely mechanically utter them without applying our whole mind to realize their fulness. "Father" is one of these words.

At Salt Lake City.

Therefore in our meditation we have to understand more deeply what it means and so to put our heart in harmony with its truth.

We can take this world as it appears to us through the medium of laws. We can have the idea of the world in our mind, as a world of force and matter, and then our relation to it becomes merely the mechanical relation of science. But, in that case, we miss the highest truth that is in man. For what is man? He is a personal being. Law does not take account of that. Law is about the physiology of our body, the psychology of our minds, the mechanism of our being. And when we come to our personal nature, we do not know any law which explains it. Therefore Science ignores the very basis of truth about ourselves. The whole world becomes a machine, and then there can be no question of looking upon the Creator as Father, or as we Indians often call him, "Mother."

If we look upon this world merely as a combination of forces, then there can be no question of worship. But we are not merely physical or psychological. We are men and women. And we must find out, in the whole world, the infinite meaning of this, that we are men.

That my body exists, Science explains by universal laws. So that I find my body to be, not an isolated fact of creation, but a part of a great whole. Then I find that even my mind thinks in harmony with all that happens in the world; and so I can find out by the help of my mind all those great laws which govern the universe.

But Science asks me to stop there. For Science, the laws of body and mind have their background in the universe, but personality has none. But we feel that we cannot accept this. For if this personality has no eternal relation to truth which everything else has, then what chimera of chance is it? Why is it at all in this world, and how? This fact of my person must have the truth of the infinite person to support it. We have come to this great discovery by the immediate perception of this "I" in us, that there must be one infinite "I."

Then comes our question, "How are we related to this Person?" Man has got this answer in his heart of heart, that it is the closest of all relationships, — the relationship of love.

It cannot be otherwise, because relationship becomes perfect only when it is that of love.

The relation of king and subject, master and servant, lawgiver and those who obey the law, — these are partial relations for one particular use. The whole being is not involved. But this personal "I" must have perfect relationship with the Infinite Personality. It cannot be otherwise. Because we have loved and find in love the infinite satisfaction of our personality, therefore we have come to know that our relationship to the Infinite Personality is that of love. And in this way man has learned to say "Our Father," not merely King, or Master, but Father.

That is to say, there is something in Him which we share, — something common between this Eternal Person and this finite little person.

But still the question remains, Why should

I use the word "Father" which represents the personal relation of human beings? Why cannot we invent another word? Is it not too finite and small?

The word Father in our Sanskrit language includes Mother. Very often we use this word in its dual form, "Pitaru," meaning "father and mother." Man is born in the arms of the Mother. We have not come merely as the rain comes from the cloud. The great fact is that I am ushered into this life in the arms of my mother and father. This shows that the idea of the personality is already there. Herein we find our relation to the Infinite Person. We know that we are born of love — our relationship is of love, and we feel that our father and mother are the true symbols of our eternal relationship with God. I have to realize this truth every moment. I have to know that I am eternally related to my Father. Then I rise above the trivialities of things, and the whole world acquires meaning for me.

Therefore the first prayer is to realize God

as Pita. Thou who createst the infinite world of stars and worlds, Thou art beyond me, but I know one thing intimately, Thou art Pita, Father.

The baby does not know all about its mother's activities, but it knows that she is its mother.

So I do not know other things about God, but I know this, Thou art my Father.

Let all my consciousness burn like fire with this idea, Thou art my Father. Every day let this be the one centre of all my thoughts, That the Supreme Person ruling all the Universe is my Father.

Pita no bodhi. Let me wake up in the light of this great truth — Thou art my Father.

Like a naked child let me place all my thoughts in Thy arms for Thy care and protection through the day.

And then Namah.

My complete self-surrender will become true. This is the highest joy of man's love.

Namaste, namah to Thee — let it be true.

I am related to the Infinite "I am" and so

my true attitude is not that of pride, or self-satisfaction, but of self-surrender. Namaste'stu.

I have not finished the whole of the text which my boys use for their prayer and meditation.

You must remember that this prayer has been gathered from different places of our oldest Scriptures — the Vedas. They are not to be found in one consecutive order in any one place. But my father, who had dedicated his life to the worship of God, collected these words from the immortal storehouse of inexhaustible wisdom — the Vedas and Upanishads.

The next line is this:

Ma ma himsi. Do not smite me with death.

We shall have fully to understand what this means. You have heard me say that in this first line it has been said, "Thou art my Father." This truth is everywhere. We have to be born into this great idea of the Father. That is the end and object of man, the fulfilment of his life.

Though it is true that we are eternally related to our Father, yet there is some barrier which prevents the full realization of this truth, and this is the greatest source of suffering to man. The animals — they have their pain, they suffer from the attacks of enemies and physical imperfection, and this suffering urges them still more to strive to fulfil the wants of their natural life and struggle against these obstacles. This in itself is a matter of joy. And we can be sure that they truly enjoy their life, because through this impulse they struggle against obstacles and this rouses their whole vitality. Otherwise they would be like the vegetable world. Life must have for its fulfilment its obstacles, and by continual fighting against these obstacles of matter, life realizes its own supremacy and dignity. But all these obstacles come to them with the accompaniment of the sensation of pain.

But with human beings there is another source of suffering still deeper. We also have to seek our livelihood and hold ourselves against all the enmities of nature and man. But that is not all. — The wonder of it is that man, being born in the same world as the animals, and having the same vital questions to deal with, still has something else for which he struggles and cares, which is not quite definitely realized. It comes to us in glimpses, and when we are in wealth, wallowing in prosperity, or luxury or ease, — when we are surrounded by all the things of the world, — still men feel that it is not sufficient for them, and there rings out the prayer, not to the natural forces of the earth, — such as air, fire, — but to some being whom man has not fully realized or known. His prayer rings out: "Save me" — "O do not smite me with death."

It is not the physical death, because we all know that we must die, and so the prayer to our Father is not for our physical immortality. Man has felt in himself instinctively that this life is not final, — that he must strive for the higher life. And then he cries to God — Do not leave me in this region of death. It does not satisfy my soul. I eat and sleep, but I am not satisfied. I do not find my good in this — I starve. As the child's cry is for the mother's food, which she supplies out of her own life, so we cry to the eternal Mother, "Do not smite me with death," but give me the life which comes out of thy own nature. — This is the cry — I am starving. My soul is smitten with death because it finds no sustenance in its surroundings.

Vishvāni deva savitar duritāni parāsuva.

O God, my Father, the world of sins remove from me. When this life of self wants to get everything for itself, then it gets knocked and knocked, because it is unnatural, because its true life is the life of freedom, because it hurts its wings against the prison cage. The Prison is unmeaning to the soul. It cries out in its prison, "I do not find my fulfilment." It knocks itself against the prison bars and from these knocks and pains our soul is fully aware that truth is not of this life of self, but of the larger life of soul. From this comes our suffering, and we say: "Break open this prison. I do not want this self." "Break all the sins, selfish desires, cravings of self, and own me as your child, — your child, not the child of this world of death."

This is the prayer when we want to realize

full consciousness of life in our Father. The greatest obstacle is the selfish life. Therefore the prayer of man to God is not for worldly goods, but for the establishment of complete relationship with the Father.

Yad bhadran tan na asuva. What is good give us.

We very often utter this prayer and ask our Father to give us what is good, but we do not know what a terrible prayer it is if we were to receive its full answer. There are very few of us who, when realizing what is the highest good, can ask for it. Only he can do that who has been able to make his life pure, free from the shackles of evil, who can fearlessly ask God to fulfil his work, who can say, "I have cleansed my mind and got rid of impulses of selfish desire and the fear and sorrow of the narrow life of self, and now I can claim with fullest hope, 'Give me what is good, in whatever form — in sorrow, loss, insult, bereavement — I shall be glad to receive it, for I know it comes from Thee.'"

But however weak we may be we have to utter

this prayer. For we know that even though we may be plunged into misery and sorrow, yet he who realizes that he lives in his Father will be glad to receive whatever comes from His hands. That is freedom. For freedom cannot be in mere pleasure. But when we can defy danger and death, privation and sorrow, and yet feel the freedom — when we have not the least doubt about the life in our Father — then everything comes with a message of gladness and we can receive it with humility and joy and bow our heads in gratitude.

"Namah sambhavāya."

"I bow to Thee from whom come the enjoyments of life." We gladly welcome these, all the different streams of joy running through various channels — and for these we bow to Thee.

"Mayobhavāya cha."

"I also bow to Thee from whom comes the welfare of man." Welfare contains in it both the joys and sorrows of life, loss and gain. To Thee who givest pain, sorrow and bereavement — to Thee I bow.

"Namah shivāya cha shivatarāya cha."

"I bow to thee who art good, who art the highest good."

This is the complete text. The first part is the prayer for consciousness that we are living not merely in the world of earth, air and water, but in the real world of personality, of love. And when we realize we are in this love — then we feel the disharmony of our lives apart from love. We do not feel it, till we are conscious of our relation to our Father. But when we are conscious, we feel the discord so strongly that it smites us and we feel it to be death. It becomes intolerable when we are in the very slightest manner conscious that we are surrounded by the love of our Father.

Then comes the prayer for freedom from things and for the highest good — *i.e.*, freedom in God.

And then comes the conclusion. We bow to Him in whom we all enjoy life, in whom is the welfare of the soul, in whom is the good.

Om, Shantih, Shantih, Shantih. Om.

WOMAN

WOMAN

When male creatures indulge in their fighting propensity to kill one another Nature connives at it, because, comparatively speaking, females are needful to her purpose, while males are barely necessary. Being of an economic disposition she does not specially care for the hungry broods who are quarrelsomely voracious and who yet contribute very little towards the payment of Nature's bill. Therefore in the insect world we witness the phenomenon of the females taking it upon themselves to keep down the male population to the bare limit of necessity.

But because greatly relieved of their responsibility to Nature, the males in the human world have had the freedom of their occupation and adventures. The definition of the human being is said to be that he is the tool-making animal. This tool-making is outside of Nature's scope. In fact, with our tool-making power we have been able to defy Nature. The human male, having the most part of his energies free, developed this power, and became formidable. Thus though in the vital department of humanity woman still occupies the throne given to her by Nature, man in the mental department has created and extended his own dominion. For this great work detachment of mind and freedom of movement were necessary.

Man took advantage of his comparative freedom from the physical and emotional bondage, and marched unencumbered towards his extension of life's boundaries. In this he has travelled through the perilous path of revolutions and ruins. Time after time his accumulations have been swept away and the current of progress has disappeared at its source. Though the gain has been considerable yet the waste in comparison has been still more enormous, especially when we consider that much of the wealth, when vanished, has taken away the records with it. Through this repeated experience of disasters man has discovered the truth, — though not fully utilized it, that in all his creations the moral rhythm has to be maintained to save them from destruction; that a mere unlimited augmentation of power does not lead to real progress, and there must be balance of proportion, must be harmony of the structure with its foundation to indicate a real growth in truth.

This ideal of stability is deeply cherished in woman's nature. She is never in love with merely going on, shooting wanton arrows of curiosity into the heart of darkness. All her forces instinctively work to bring things to some shape of fulness, — for that is the law of life. In life's movement though nothing is final yet every step has its rhythm of completeness. Even the bud has its ideal of rounded perfection, so has the flower, and also the fruit. But an unfinished building has not that ideal of wholeness in itself. Therefore if it goes on indefinitely in its growth of dimensions, it gradually grows out of its standard of stability. The masculine creations of intellectual civilization are towers of Babel, they dare to defy their foundations and therefore topple down over and over again. Thus human history is growing up over layers of ruins; it is not a continuous life growth. The present war is an illustration of this. The economic and political organizations, which merely represent mechanical power, born of intellect, are apt to forget their centres of gravity in the foundational world of life. The cumulative greed of power and possession which can have no finality of completeness in itself, which has no harmony with the ideal of moral and spiritual perfection, must at last lay a violent hand upon its own ponderousness of material.

At the present stage of history civilization is almost exclusively masculine, a civilization of power, in which woman has been thrust aside in the shade. Therefore it has lost its balance and it is moving by hopping from war to war. Its motive forces are the forces of destruction and its ceremonials are carried through an appalling number of human sacrifices. This one-sided civilization is crashing along a series of catastrophes at a tremendous speed because of its one-sidedness. And at last the time has arrived when woman must step in and impart her life rhythm into this reckless movement of power.

For woman's function is the passive function of the soil which not only helps the tree to grow but keeps its growth within limits. The tree must have life's adventure and send up and spread out its branches on all sides, but all its deeper bonds of relation are hidden and held firm in the soil and this helps it to live. Our civilization must also have its passive element broad and deep and stable. It must not be mere growth but harmony of growth. It must not be all tune but it must have its time also. This time is not a barrier, it is what the banks are to the river; they guide its current into permanence, which otherwise would lose itself into the amorphousness of morass. It is rhythm, the rhythm which does not check the world's movements but leads them into truth and beauty.

Woman is endowed with the passive qualities of chastity, modesty, devotion and power of self-sacrifice in a greater measure than man is.

It is the passive quality in nature which turns its monster forces into perfect creations of beauty — taming the wild elements into the delicacy of tenderness fit for the service of life. This passive quality has given woman that large and deep placidity which is so necessary for the healing and nourishing and storing of life. If life were all spending, then it would be like a rocket, going up in a flash and coming down the next moment in ashes. Life should be like a lamp where the potentiality of light is far greater in quantity than what appears as the flame. It is in the depth of passiveness in woman's nature that this potentiality of life is stored.

I have said elsewhere that in the women of the Western world a certain restlessness is noticed which cannot be the normal aspect of her nature. For women who want something special and violent in their surroundings to keep their interests active only prove that they have lost touch with their own true world. Apparently, numbers of women as well as men in the West condemn the things that are commonplace.

They are always hankering after something which is out of the common, straining their powers to produce a spurious originality that merely surprises though it may not satisfy. But such efforts are not a real sign of vitality. And they must be more injurious to women than to men, because women have the vital power more strongly in them than men have. They are the mothers of the race, and they have a real interest in the things that are around them, that are the common things of life; if they did not have that, then the race would perish.

If, by constantly using outside stimulation, they form something like a mental drug habit, become addicted to a continual dram-drinking of sensationalism, then they lose the natural high sensibility which they have, and with it the bloom of their womanhood, and their real power to sustain the human race with what it needs the lost.

A man's interest in his fellow-beings becomes real when he finds in them some special gift of power or usefulness, but a woman feels interest in her fellow-beings because they are living creatures, because they are human, not because of some particular purpose which they can serve, or some power which they possess and for which she has a special admiration. And because woman has this power, she exercises such charm over our minds; her exuberance of vital interest is so attractive that it makes her speech, her laughter, her movement, everything graceful; for the note of gracefulness is in this harmony with all our surrounding interests.

Fortunately for us, our everyday world has the subtle and unobtrusive beauty of the commonplace, and we have to depend upon our own sensitive minds to realize its wonders which are invisible because spiritual. If we can pierce through the exterior, we find that the world in its commonplace aspects is a miracle.

We realize this truth intuitively through our power of love; and women, through this power, discover that the object of their love and sympathy, in spite of its ragged disguise of triviality, has infinite worth. When women have lost the power of interest in things that are common, then leisure frightens them with its emptiness, because their natural sensibilities being deadened, there is nothing in their surroundings to occupy their attention. Therefore they keep themselves frantically busy, not in utilizing the time, but merely in filling it up. Our everyday world is like a reed, its true value is not in itself, — but those who have the power and the serenity of attention can hear the music which the Infinite plays through its very emptiness. But when they form the habit of valuing things for themselves, then they may be expected furiously to storm your mind, to decoy your soul from her love-tryst of the eternal and to make you try to smother the voice of the Infinite by the unmeaning rattle of ceaseless movement.

I do not mean to imply that domestic life is the only life for a woman. I mean that the human world is the woman's world, be it domestic or be it full of the other activities of life which are human activities, and not merely abstract efforts to organize.

Wherever there is something which is concretely personal and human, there is woman's world. The domestic world is the world where every individual finds his worth as an individual, therefore his value is not the market value, but the value of love; that is to say, the value that God in His infinite mercy has set upon all His creatures. This domestic world has been the gift of God to woman. She can extend her radiance of love beyond its boundaries on all sides, and even leave it to prove her woman's nature when the call comes to her. But this is a truth which cannot be ignored, that the moment she is born in her mother's arms, she is born in the centre of her own true world, the world of human relationships.

Woman should use her power to break through the surface and go to the centre of things, where in the mystery of life dwells an eternal source of interest. Man has not this power to such an extent. But woman has it, if she does not kill it, — and therefore she loves creatures who are not lovable for their uncommon qualities. Man has to do his duty in a world of his own where he is always creating power and wealth and organizations of different kinds. But God has sent woman to love the world, which is a world of ordinary things and events. She is not in the world of the fairy-tale where the fair woman sleeps for ages till she is touched by the magic wand. In God's world women have their magic wands everywhere, which keeps their hearts awake, — and these are not the golden wands of wealth nor the iron rods of power.

All our spiritual teachers have proclaimed the infinite worth of the individual. It is the rampant materialism of the present age which ruthlessly sacrifices individuals to the bloodthirsty idols of organization. When religion was materialistic, when men worshipped their gods for fear of their malevolence, or for greed of wealth and power, then the ceremonies of worship were cruel and sacrifices were claimed without number. With the growth of man's spiritual life, our worship has become the worship of love.

At the present stage of civilization, when the mutilation of individuals is not only practised, but glorified, women are feeling ashamed of their own womanliness. For God, with his message of love, has sent them as guardians of individuals, and, in this their divine vocation, individuals are more to them than army and navy and parliament, shops and factories. Here they have their service in God's own temple of reality, where love is of more value than power.

But because men in their pride of power have taken to deriding things that are living and relationships that are human, a large number of women are screaming themselves hoarse to prove that they are not women, that they are true where they represent power and organization. In the present age they feel that their pride is hurt when they are taken as mere mothers of the race, as the ministers to the vital needs of its existence, and to its deeper spiritual necessity of sympathy and love.

Because men praise with pious unctuousness the idolatry of their manufactured images of abstractions, women in shame are breaking their own true God, who is waiting for His worship of self-sacrifice in love.

Changes have been going on for a long time underneath the solid crust of society on which woman's world has its foundation. Of late, with the help of science, civilization has been growing increasingly masculine, from which the full reality of the individual is more and more ignored. Organization is encroaching upon the province of personal relationship, and sentiment is giving way to law. In some societies, too much dominated by masculine ideals, infanticide prevailed, which ruthlessly kept down the female element of the population as low as possible. The same thing in another form has taken place in modern civilization. In its inordinate lust for power and wealth it has robbed woman of the most part of her world, and the home is every day being crowded out by the office. It is taking the whole world for itself, leaving hardly any room for woman. It is not merely inflicting injury but insult upon her.

But woman cannot be pushed back for good into the mere region of the decorative by man's aggressiveness of power. For she is not less necessary in civilization than man but possibly more so. In the geological history of earth the periods of gigantic cataclysms have passed when the earth had not attained her mellowness of maturity which despises all violent exhibition of force. And the civilization of competing commerce and fighting powers must also make room for that stage of perfection whose power lies deep in beauty and beneficence. So long it has been ambition which was at the helm of our history, and therefore every right of the individual had to be wrenched by force from the party in power and man has had to invoke the help of evil to attain what was good for him. But such arrangement cannot last for long, it must give way time after time; for the seeds of violence lie in wait in its cracks and crevices, and roots of disruption spread in the dark and cause breakdown when it is least expected.

Therefore although in the present stage of

history man is asserting his masculine supremacy and building his civilization with stone blocks, ignoring the living principle of growth, he cannot altogether crush woman's nature into dust or into his dead building materials. Woman's home may have been shattered, but woman is not, and cannot, herself be killed. It is not that woman is merely seeking her freedom of livelihood, struggling against man's monopoly of business, but against man's monopoly of civilization where he is breaking her heart every day and desolating her life. She must restore the lost social balance by putting the full weight of the woman into the creation of the human world. The monster car of organization is creaking and growling along life's highway, spreading misery and mutilation, for it must have speed before everything else in the world. Therefore woman must come into the bruised and maimed world of the individuals; she must claim each one of them as her own, the useless and the insignificant. She must protect under her care all the beautiful flowers of sentiments from the scorching laughter of the science of proficiency. The growing impurities, born of life's deprivation of its normal conditions imposed upon it by the organized power of greed, she must sweep away. The time has come when woman's responsibility has become greater than ever before, when her field of work has far transcended the domestic sphere of life. The world with its insulted individuals has sent its appeal to her. These individuals must find their true value, raise their heads once again in the sun, and renew their faith in God's love through her love.

Men have seen the absurdity of to-day's civilization, which is based upon nationalism, — that is to say, on economics and politics and its consequent militarism. Men have been losing their freedom and their humanity in order to fit themselves for vast mechanical organizations. So the next civilization, it is hoped, will be based not merely upon economical and political competition and exploitation, but upon world-wide social coöperation; upon spiritual ideals of reciprocity, and not upon economic ideals of efficiency. And then women will have their true place.

Because men have been building up vast and monstrous organizations they have got into the habit of thinking that this turning out power has something of the nature of perfection in itself. The habit is ingrained in them, and it is difficult for them to see where truth is missing in this present ideal of progress.

But woman can bring her fresh mind and all her power of sympathy to this new task of building up a spiritual civilization, if she will be conscious of her responsibilities. Of course, she can be frivolous or very narrow in her outlook, and then she will miss her great mission. And just because woman has been insulated, has been living in a sort of obscurity, behind man, I think she will have her compensation in the civilization which is waiting to come.

And these human beings who have been boastful of their power, and aggressive in their exploitation, who have lost faith in the real meaning of the teaching of their Master, that the meek shall inherit the earth, will be defeated in the next generation of life. It is the same thing that happened in the ancient days, in the prehistoric times, to those great monsters like the mammoths and dinosaurs. They have lost their inheritance of the earth. They had the gigantic muscles for mighty efforts but they had to give up to creatures who were much feebler in their muscles and who took up much less space with their dimensions. And in the future civilization also, the women, the feebler creatures, — feebler at least in their outer aspects, — who are less muscular, and who have been behindhand, always left under the shadow of those huge creatures, the men, — they will have their place, and those bigger creatures will have to give way.